Doggie Knits

Sweaters & Accessories for Your Best Friend

CORINNE NIESSNER

STERLING

New York / London
www.sterlingpublishing.com

STERLING and the distinctive Sterling logo are registered trademarks of Sterling Publishing Co., Inc.

Library of Congress Cataloging-in-Publication Data

Niessner, Corinne.
    Doggie knits : sweaters & accessories for your best friend / Corinne Niessner.
        p. cm.
    Includes index.
    ISBN-13: 978-1-4027-3069-6
    ISBN-10: 1-4027-3069-1
    1. Knitting--Patterns. 2. Dogs--Equipment and supplies. I. Title.
    TT825.N5155 2008
    746.43'2041--dc22

2007012473

The Little Penny sweater pattern originally appeared in the online magazine *Knitty* in Fall 2003.

10 9 8 7 6 5 4 3 2

Published by Sterling Publishing Co., Inc.
387 Park Avenue South, New York, NY 10016
©2008 by Corinne Niessner
Distributed in Canada by Sterling Publishing
c/o Canadian Manda Group, 165 Dufferin Street
Toronto, Ontario, Canada M6K 3H6
Distributed in the United Kingdom by GMC Distribution Services
Castle Place, 166 High Street, Lewes, East Sussex, England BN7 1XU
Distributed in Australia by Capricorn Link (Australia) Pty. Ltd.
P.O. Box 704, Windsor, NSW 2756, Australia

Book design and layout: Scott Meola, Simplissimus
How-to illustrations: Orrin Lundgren

Printed in China
All rights reserved

Sterling ISBN-13: 978-1-4027-3069-6
       ISBN-10: 1-4027-3069-1

For information about custom editions, special sales, premium and corporate purchases, please contact Sterling Special Sales Department at 800-805-5489 or specialsales@sterlingpublishing.com.

Gratitude

Many thanks to the following people who supported *Doggie Knits*:

- Jo Fagan, my editor at Sterling Publishing. I had always thought about writing a book in the distant future, and you helped make my dream come true.

- Isabel Stein and the Design team at Sterling Publishing, for taking my raw components and making them into a book. I've learned so much from you.

- David Christensen, my very dear friend. Your photography is as beautiful as I had imagined. You put so much of your heart into this project.

- Josh Gage and Keith Sawyer, thank you for helping us marry technology with art in the making of photos for this book.

- Clarence Towers and the San Francisco Recreation and Park Department Photography Center, our most gracious hosts for the photo shoots.

- Trish Watson, thank you for finding so many lovely dogs to model for this book.

- Hollus Gessler and Travis Thomas, thank you for helping me with the photos.

- Judy Chan, thank you for sample knitting and helping with the Astro pattern.

- Linda Ellis, thanks for testing the Gidget design.

- Bonnie Marie Burns, my good friend and mentor. Thank you for making Lucky Penny's Internet presence so beautiful.

- Pamela Menas and Lee Mann, who helped me adopt my first dog, and got me down this path of being a pet lover.

- My muse Piccolo, who provides inspiration every day and the memory of my departed pets: Yoda, Penny, and Gidget Alice.

- The Man, D, who keeps every day silly.

A special thanks to the lovely pets who made the designs come to life, and their human companions:

- Wendie B., and Woodie

- Sara and Scott Bell, and Co-pilot

- Roz Coloma–Guerrero, and Laroz Little Boy Blue and Robrex Kinsington (aka Kinsey)

- Diane Choplin and Jonathan Claassen, and Skye

- Son Dang, and Butter and Peanut

- Michael Hamlin, and Penny

- Kody Hilton, and Mr. Lucky

- Cindy Kahl, and Buttercup and Lincoln

- Lonnie Leonard, and Lyubi

- Clint Otwell, and Rita

- Cynthia Preciado, and Chico

- Ellen Sherrod, and Picante Buendia "Pica"

- Paulino Tamayo, and Zoey and ZeeNa

- Klaudia Warren, and Romeo Princeton

- Patricia Watson, and Bee and Teddy, Cairn terriers

Why Dog Sweaters?

My dog Piccolo is curled up next to me as I knit a project. This is her happiest place, where she is fulfilling what she feels is her duty and purpose in life. *To be with me.* She may also want something good to eat, or a squeaky toy, but what she wants most is *to be with me*. Is there any one more deserving of my knitting?

My history with dog sweaters began some years ago, when I adopted my first dog. I had been a lifelong knitter and I almost immediately began knitting for Yoda. As an experienced knitter, I was comfortable with tweaking a design. An element here, an element there, to obtain the best fit. Then I started adding elements of color. I added an edge here and there, to define the lines of the sweater design. The more unexpected the color, the better I liked it. Over the years, I said my sad farewells to my beloved dogs Yoda, Penny, and Gidget Alice; all of them, who most of all wanted *to be with me*, were my little muses.

The dog sweater is a small, satisfying project that can be accomplished in the same amount of time it takes to knit a hat, scarf, or mittens. These projects can be taken with you for a trip, or used for a commuter or knitting group project. The lovely thing is that you will be finished with the sweater long before the project gets tedious or boring. The yarn requirements are generally small. A sweater can be knit using leftovers from larger projects, or can be made of a luxury fiber that you may not want to splurge on for a sweater for yourself.

Dogs are the unique creatures who were engineered by humans for companionship. They are on this earth *to be with us*. Having a dog in our home is the most sacred privilege.

Celebrate the bond you have with your dog with your knitting! I hope this book will help you accomplish just that.

Contents

Romeo Princeton in a Piccolo sweater.

Celebrate Your Dog

The sweater designs in this book are classic. They are based on the essential elements needed for a sweater your dog will want to wear. They are simple in shape, but not simple in design. The sweaters are not overly cute or gimmicky; their beauty comes from impeccable fit, attention to detail, a fresh approach to color, and the best materials available.

A Sweater Your Dog Will Want to Wear

I heard someone tell the story of her little dog Shorty, who was always dressed in a sweater to run outside. He would always return home without the sweater. His family would buy him a new sweater and send Shorty outside again, only to have him return home again without the sweater. The next spring, Shorty's family found the sweaters buried in the backyard. Shorty wiggled out of them, apparently, and hid them so as not to have to wear one again. Shorty clearly had an uncomfortable sweater. A well-fitting sweater, made with a quality fiber, will be a garment that a dog will want to wear. It will provide much-needed protection from the elements, and a layer of warmth needed by small dogs, as well as older or ill dogs.

Choosing the right materials is essential to the success of any project. In the case of the dog sweater, consider how it will be used. If your pet is what I refer to as a pocket dog, a pet so small that it can be carried in one hand or handbag, a luxury fiber

Woodie in a hooded sweater.

such as a cashmere or alpaca is a fine choice. If you can find these fibers blended with wool, your finished garment will hold its shape better with frequent wear. Tiny sweaters, not requiring much yarn, are a worthy splurge for a luxury material that might be cost prohibitive if making a sweater for a larger dog.

A sweater that a dog will be wearing for outside walks requires using a fiber that can really stand up to heavy wear and frequent washings. Your dog, being relatively low to the ground, will get a sweater soiled more quickly than you would with regular wear. My first choice is always wool, or wool blended with mohair. These yarns don't have to be the most expensive available. In fact, what I use most often are yarns that are available in most local shops, ones that offer a wide color range and happen to be inexpensive. My choice is to not use machine washable wool. I have found that with frequent wearing and washing, the sweaters fall apart after one season. I don't recommend using all synthetic yarns, as most may be easy care, but really won't keep your dog warm. Except for summerwear for sun protection, cotton is not a good choice for sweaters, as it won't keep warm when wet, as wool will.

A dog sweater may require a few washings per season and, to prevent moth infestation, it should always be cleaned before being put away for the warm season. I use a detergent made for wool or a mild shampoo and let it soak for fifteen to twenty minutes; then I rinse thoroughly. To get the excess water out I use the spin cycle of my washing machine. The sweaters can also be put in a salad spinner or rolled in a clean towel. Dry the sweaters flat on a clean towel, away from direct sunlight.

Fitting the sweater to our dog is the most important aspect in achieving a comfortable sweater. To choose the correct size of sweater to make you will need to know a few measurements as shown opposite. Measure your dog and adjust the pattern if necessary.

Attention to detail will take your project from looking home-made to handmade. The patterns in this book have some features that will give that special touch to your sweater.

1. The selvedge: I prefer a selvedge for smooth seaming and picked up edges. The one I prefer is to slip the first stitch of every row, and knit the last stitch of every row.

MEASURING YOUR DOG

The Harness Hole: You can make a harness hole, an optional knit-in buttonhole opening that will allow the dog to wear a harness under the sweater. To locate the hole, measure from the back of the neck to where the D-ring is placed on the harness.

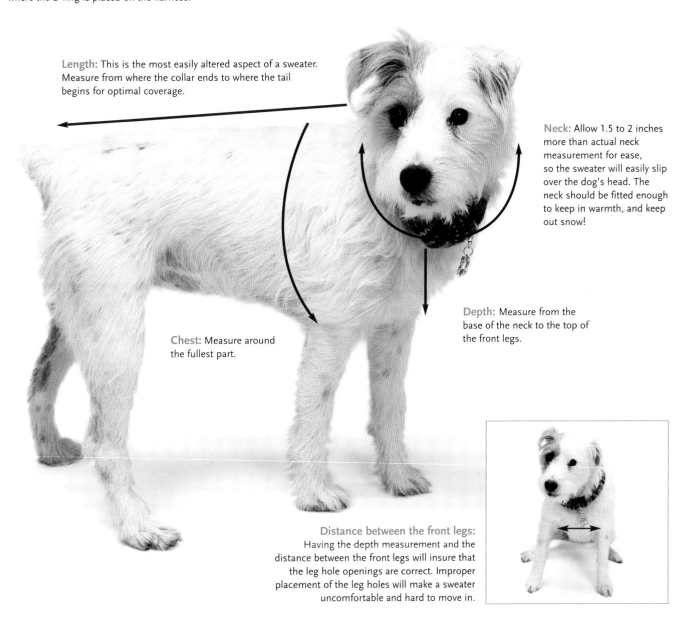

Length: This is the most easily altered aspect of a sweater. Measure from where the collar ends to where the tail begins for optimal coverage.

Neck: Allow 1.5 to 2 inches more than actual neck measurement for ease, so the sweater will easily slip over the dog's head. The neck should be fitted enough to keep in warmth, and keep out snow!

Chest: Measure around the fullest part.

Depth: Measure from the base of the neck to the top of the front legs.

Distance between the front legs: Having the depth measurement and the distance between the front legs will insure that the leg hole openings are correct. Improper placement of the leg holes will make a sweater uncomfortable and hard to move in.

3

2. Directional decreases: Having the decreases move in the direction of the work lends a more professional look. I use a knit two together (k2tog) decrease to slant right, and a slip, slip, knit decrease to slant left.

3. Short rows: I find that using short rows in the body shaping near the tail results in a better fit and a better looking ribbed body band.

If you are knitting a sweater for a gift, you may not know, or be able to obtain, the exact measurements of the recipient. Some possibilities are the Penny sweaters which allow for a lot of stretch, or the Agnes sweater, which ties at the neck. Alternatively, you could knit a Libby kerchief or a home gift such as the Lyubi blanket, the Wally bed, or the Chickies toy.

Play with Color

I knit custom sweaters; at times I have offered yarns displayed from my massive stash for the customers to choose, only to have their first choice be gray. Their choice for the turtleneck and body bands was: another gray. I convinced them to choose a bright color for the trim to add interest to the sweater. Knitters, please stay away from the gray! Part of the fun of knitting dog sweaters for me is to combine colors in new ways, and one combination usually sparks even more ideas.

Over the years of knitting dog sweaters, I developed a few rules for approaching color. These rules are not based on any sort of theory or science; I find that overanalyzing color choices takes the fun out of it for me.

RULE 1. **Choosing colors for your sweaters should be approached as a fun activity.** Touching yarn, smelling it, and drinking in the color is a delightful experience. I think about the how the colors relate to each other. I also think about the relationship that the colors of the yarn have to the color of the dog.

RULE 2. **Consider what colors would look good on your dog.** Some thoughts:

▶ For little dogs, choose bright colors for safety.

▶ White dogs can wear any color and look good!

A turquoise body with magenta and pumpkin cuffs makes Zoey easy to spot.

▶ Black dogs can wear really strong, bright colors.

▶ Brown dogs would look good in pink, yellow, red, and turquoise.

▶ Red dogs: green and purples would look good.

What I have done with my own dogs over the years was to have a special color that was theirs for collars, leashes, and garments. A garment with many colors would have the pet's signature color in it. This idea is useful for a household with multiple pets of the same size, so you can tell the sweaters apart.

RULE 3. **Expand your idea of neutral colors. Blue, green, and brown can all work as neutrals.** Any color can be worn with blue jeans; think of blue wool in the same way. Every flower arrangement needs greenery, and green is everywhere in nature, as is brown. Use all these colors with pinks, yellows, orange, and purple for really interesting combinations. If you need color inspiration, a trip to a botanic garden, florist, aquarium, or even a produce section of a grocery store can become a color story for your sweater. Use a piece of art whose colors speak to you as your inspiration.

For little dogs, choose bright colors. These sweaters were made in shades of pink, blue, and orange for the bodies. Complementary colors were used for the body bands, leg holes, and collars.

A variegated pink sweater is adorable on Pilot, the pug puppy, and goes with the dog's coloring.

Orange edges are a sharp contrast for a beautiful sweater in stripes of blues and purples.

Blue and burgundy variegated yarns were used for the body, with collars, legs, and body bands of olive, purple, pumpkin, and turquoise.

Gold and two shades of green are a fresh approach to autumnal color.

One of my favorite combinations has been what has been named the Sock Monkey sweater. It is a simple black and white sweater, knit with a black and gray ragg type wool for the body, with bands in black, white, or gray. What makes the sweater unique and interesting is the color choices for the neck and band edges. I have used either one bright color for the edges, or for a really great effect, a different bright color for each of the edges. Using different edge colors also became a design feature in the Shadow sweater design in this book.

RULE 4. Play with stripes. I love self-striping yarn, and it seems that more are available every day. For a dog sweater, I generally use the stripes for the body piece, and consider it to be one color when picking yarns for the sweater. If making a flat body piece, work the each small inner leg section first, so the stripes match up when the garment is seamed. The leg and body bands and collar can be knit with a solid color pulled from the striped section. For a really great effect, choose an unexpected color for the edges.

RULE 5. Take risks with hand-painted yarns. I love hand-painted yarns. The depth of color and the unusual combinations that can be found really resonate with me. While I find that I cannot wear most for a garment larger than an accessory piece, these yarns make really special dog sweaters. One of the risks, or surprises, depending on your point of view, is when one color tends to pool together on the knitted garment. Some manufacturers suggest alternating two rows from each of two balls of yarn. I tend to not do this, and just let the colors pool randomly as most of the time the effect does not bother me. I also love to combine different colors of hand-painted yarns for my body and band knitting. If each of the hand-painted yarns used have one color in common, the combination will look good.

RULE 6. Use three colors. One day, it just happened. I was playing with my yarn stash, combining body and band colors for sweaters, and just thought to pepper my combination with a third, accent color. It was magic, and became the cornerstone of most of my design work. Adding the third, often unrelated, color, seemed to make the other two colors sing. I'm not certain if a three color combination is based on academic theory or study, but a friend tells me that odd-numbered color combinations appear to be more pleasing to the eye. Some basic combinations can use a bright-colored edge, such as orange or yellow, with a combination of blues, greens, or purples on the body and bands. Or try a hot blue or green edge on red and pink body and band combinations. When I look at color combinations that please me in art, advertising, or gardening, I try to pull out three colors that appeal to me and would make a beautiful sweater.

Bright bands, trim, and buttons add interest to neutral blues and browns.

Yellow tips add spark to a cozy sweater in shades of tan, gray, and brown.

Orange, purple, blue, and green add contrast to a pink palette.

Warm pinks and oranges make this sweater special.

Adding bright colors at the edges gives punch to what would otherwise be a neutral palette.

Mr. Lucky models a ragg wool Sock Monkey sweater accented with magenta, black, turquoise, and orange.

Orange and yellow trim bring life to a neutral color palette.

Woodie models a sweater with stripes in warm pinks and earth tones.

Dyeing Your Own Yarns

If you don't have hand-painted yarns available yet really like the effect, you could try dyeing your own at home. I like using unsweetened powdered drink mixes. This is a great method for small projects, and since you are working with a food product, you can safely use your kitchen utensils for this process. The yarn is dyed with a combination of the acid in the drink mix, and heat. This process only works with animal fibers.

▶ To dye your own, prepare white, or any color yarn you would like to dye, by winding in small hanks, tied loosely with scrap yarn to prevent tangling.

▶ Soak the hanks in water for at least one hour.

▶ Mix one package of drink mix into hot tap water for every ounce of yarn to be dyed.

▶ Twist the hanks for a tie-dyed effect. Place the hanks and the drink mix into a large clear jar with a lid, and pour in hot water, and just let things sit.

▶ The process is done when the water is clear. You can repeat this as often as you like, twisting the yarn hanks in the reverse direction.

Another method to add color on top of the tie dyed yarn is to paint on the drink dye with a sponge. Use gloves for this step, to prevent staining hands. With the yarn hanks in a microwave dish, dab on the color using the sponge. Place the dish in the microwave and heat for one minute to set the dye. The water in the pan will be clear when the dye is set. When the yarn is dyed, wash the hanks in a mild shampoo, and allow them to dry. The result will be beautiful, one of a kind yarn that can be mixed with solids or other hand paints for any project in this book. The photos on page 10 show hanks of hand-dyed yarn.

Place the prepared yarn in the dye bath.

The dye bath will be clear when all the color is absorbed.

Add layers of additional color by applying dye with a sponge.

Designer Notes about the Patterns

▸ Yarn amounts to complete the projects in the book are an approximation. Purchase extra to avoid disappointment. Yarn shops often accept skeins of unused yarn as returns or exchanges. Yarn weights for projects are specified rather than brand names, so the knitter can choose from products available locally.

▸ Directions are written with the needle sizes that I used to obtain gauge. We used US sizing of needles throughout (metric is given in parenthesis). I knit loosely, so the tighter knitters out there may need to go up a few needle sizes to achieve the same gauge.

▸ Read the directions completely before starting a project to familiarize yourself with the skills needed to complete a design. Consult the techniques section of the book if necessary.

▸ Whenever possible, the patterns are written to use a selvedge stitch. My opinion is that it makes for easier, smoother seaming of the garments and a neater edge for picking up stitches.

▸ For many of the projects, circular needles are used even if the knitting is worked flat. I like the fact that the cable can serve as a stitch holder for the sections not being worked. In my opinion, having the project on one needle also makes it more portable.

KNITTING ABBREVIATIONS

Here is a list of abbreviations used in the patterns.

BO	bind off	**PSSO**	pass slipped stitch over
CC	contrast color	**PU**	pick up
CO	cast on	**RIB**	ribbing
CDD	center double decrease	**RS**	right side of garment
DPN	double-pointed needle	**SL**	slip
K	knit	**ST**	stitch
K2tog	knit two together	**SSK**	slip, slip, knit
M1	make one increase	**TBL**	through the back loop
MC	main color	**TOG**	together
P	purl	**WS**	wrong side of garment
PM	place marker	**YO**	yarn over

* *Directions appearing between the asterisks should be repeated across row, as many times as specified in the pattern.

Circular arrows on a schematic indicate that that part of the garment was knitted in the round.

Sizes: Regarding measurements, schematics are drawn *without* the ribbed body band, which is added after the sweater is seamed. The length of the sweater piece knitted flat is 1 1/2 inches shorter than the total body length will be once the band is added (if pattern calls for a body band). Knitting needles are given in US sizes, with metric sizes in parenthesis (see page 89 for needle chart).

Hand-dyed yarn in bright colors. When winding the hand-painted yarn, divide into 2 balls; then knit two rows from each, alternating to prevent pooling.

More hand-dyed yarn in warm tones. Two hand-painted yarns with green trim would make a colorful sweater.

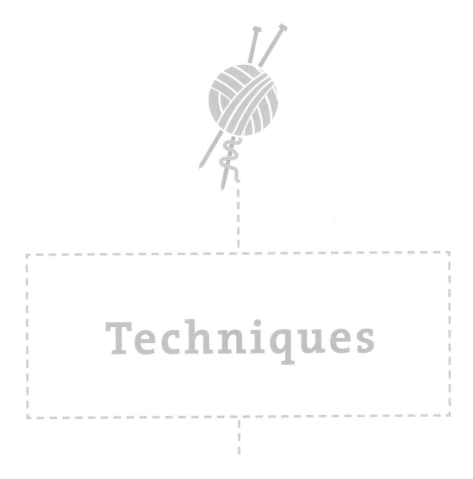

Techniques

Knitting is always the process of moving a set of stitches from a left-hand needle to a right-hand needle, creating a fabric. This is a skill that, once learned, always has the potential to get better. I will admit to being a better knitter now than I was decades ago, and not as good as I will be years from now. These are basic maneuvers that will take you through most of the projects in the book. I would encourage you to seek the company of others who share your enthusiasm for knitting. Observing what others are working on is something I find inspiring. It is always helpful to find instruction at your local yarn shop, park district, or knitting guild.

Casting on

Backward loop cast on

Make slip knot and insert working needle into loop. Holding working needle in your right hand, wrap working yarn around your left thumb (T1-1). Insert needle under yarn nearest to you, and lift off stitch (T1-2, T1-3). Repeat for desired number of stitches.

T1-1 Put slip knot on needle and wrap long loose end of yarn around thumb.

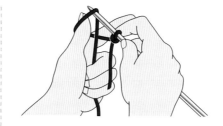

T1-2 Insert needle through the strand of yarn on your thumb.

T1-3 Slip the loop from your thumb to the needle, pulling to tighten. Repeat until desired number of stitches are on the needle.

Long-tail cast on

This cast on has the advantage of working one row of knitting, so your work will always begin on the wrong side. Measure off yarn three times the intended width of your garment. Make slip knot and fasten on to needle. Holding the needle in your right hand, wrap the tail yarn around your left thumb and the working yarn around your forefinger (T2-1). Insert needle under tail yarn, creating a loop (T2-2) and draw working yarn through loop creating a stitch (T2-3). Repeat for desired number of stitches.

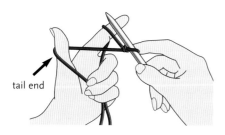

tail end

T2-1 Make a slip knot on the needle; leaving a tail that is as long as about three times the width of the piece to be knitted. Wind the tail yarn around your left thumb from front to back. Wrap the working yarn over your left index finger, and secure both ends in your palm.

T2-2 Insert the needle upwards in the loop on your thumb; then, using the needle draw the working yarn through the loop to form the stitch.

T2-3 Remove your thumb from the loop and tighten the loop on the needle. Repeat until you have cast on the desired number of stitches.

Knitted cast on

For the designs in this book, the knitted cast on is used to create leg holes and can be chosen for making a buttonhole. Insert right-hand needle into first stitch on left-hand needle as if to knit (T3-1). Draw yarn through as if to knit and place loop on to left-hand needle (T3-2, T3-3). Repeat for desired number of stitches.

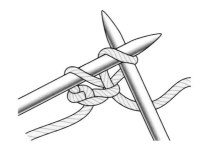

T3-1 Make a slip knot on the left-hand needle. Insert the right needle into the loop knitwise, wrapping the working yarn around the right needle as if to knit.

T3-2 Draw the working yarn through as if to knit, leaving the loop on the left-hand needle.

T3-3 Move the new loop over to the left-hand needle. Repeat until you have cast on the desired number of stitches.

Cable cast on

Work two stitches on to left-hand needle using knitted method. For additional stitches, insert the right-hand needle between the first two stitches on the left-hand needle (T4-1), draw working yarn through (T4-2), and place new stitch on left-hand needle (T4-3).

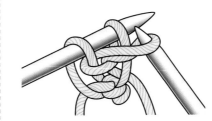

T4-1 Cast on two stitches as in the knitted cast on method. Insert the right-hand needle between the two stitches.

T4-2 Wrap the yarn around the right-hand needle as if to knit, and draw the yarn through, creating a new stitch.

T4-3 Transfer the new stitch to the left-hand needle. Repeat until you have the desired number of stitches, always inserting the right-hand needle through the last two stitches on the left-hand needle.

Provisional cast on

This cast on is used if leaving live stitches to be worked later is desired. Using waste yarn and a crochet hook, chain desired number of stitches plus 5 to 10 extra. Tie a knot in the end of waste yarn to mark which side to open up when needed. With working yarn, knit into back loop of chains for desired number of stitches (T5-1). To rip, undo yarn at knotted end of chain and pull, placing all loose stitches on knitting needle as you go (T5-2).

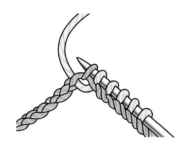

T5-1 Using waste yarn (blue) and a crochet hook, make a chain that is slightly longer than the number of stitches to cast on. Pull working yarn through the back of the chain loops, leaving stitches on the needle.

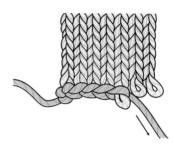

T5-2 When piece is worked to completion, and you want to knit in the other direction, unravel the waste yarn, exposing live stitches to be placed on a needle.

Knit stitch and other stitches

Knit (k)

With stitches on left-hand needle, insert right-hand needle into nearest stitch, from front to back, creating an X shape with left-hand needle over right (T6-1). Wrap working yarn, from back to front, around right-hand needle (T6-2). Using right-hand needle, pull working yarn through stitch (T6-3), and pull left-hand needle out, moving stitch over to right-hand needle (T6-4).

T6-1 Insert the right-hand needle from front to back into the first loop on the left-hand needle. Hold the yarn in back of the work.

T6-2 Wrap the yarn around the right-hand needle.

T6-3 Using the right-hand needle, draw the yarn through the loop.

T6-4 Slip the stitch off the left-hand needle, leaving the newly created stitch on the right-hand needle.

Knitting through the back loop (ktbl)

Knitting through the back of the loop creates a twisted stitch than can be used to create an interesting texture for some of the projects in the book. Insert right-hand needle into the part of the stitch on the left-hand needle that is farthest away from you, working on the stitch nearest the tip of the left-hand needle (T7-1). Wrap working yarn from back to front, around right-hand needle. Using right-hand needle, pull working yarn through stitch, and pull left-hand needle out, moving stitch over to right-hand needle.

T7-1 Wrap the yarn around the right-hand needle, and draw through the loop. Slip the loop off the left-hand needle, leaving the newly created stitch on the right-hand needle.

Purl (p)

Hold yarn in front of work. Insert right-hand needle into front of stitch on left-hand needle (T8-1). Wrap yarn around right-hand needle (T8-2) and pull through loop on left-hand needle, moving stitch over to right-hand needle (T8-3).

T8-1 Insert the right-hand needle from back to front into the first loop on the left-hand needle. The working yarn is held in front.

T8-2 Wrap the yarn around the right-hand needle in a counterclockwise motion.

T8-3 Draw the yarn through the loop, and then drop the loop from the left-hand needle. The newly created purl stitch is on the right-hand needle.

Slip stitch (sl st)

Pass stitch from left-hand needle to right-hand needle without working it. This may be done knitwise (T9-1) or purlwise (T9-2).

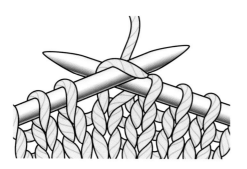

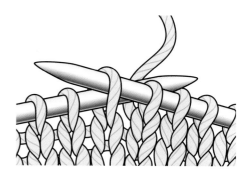

T9-1 Move a stitch from the left needle to the right needle as if to knit.

T9-2 Move a stitch from the left needle to the right needle as if to purl.

Make one increase (m1)

I think this method makes the smoothest increase; it is the chosen method for the projects in this book. Using left-hand needle, lift bar on stitch between tip of left and right needle (T10-1) and twist it onto left-hand needle (T10-2) to become a stitch. Knit or purl stitch as desired (T10-3).

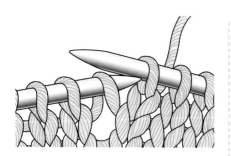

T10-1 Lift the bar between stitches on the left and right-hand needles, using the left-hand needle and leaving the loop on the left-hand needle.

T10-2 Knit the new loop through the back to twist it.

T10-3 If making the increase on a purl side, purl the loop through the back.

Yarn over (yo)

This type of increase makes of hole in your knitting. It is used for lace and edging. Lay working yarn over right-hand needle, from back to front. Then position yarn to work the next stitch. If the next stitch is knit, move working yarn to back (T11-1).

If the next stitch is purled, leave the working yarn in front (T11-2). On the following row, the yarn that has been laid over the needle is worked as a stitch.

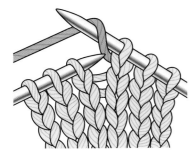

T11-1 Bring the yarn to the front, and then knit the next stitch in the normal way.

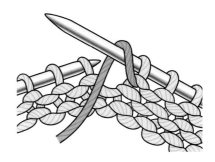

T11-2 On the next row, work the newly created loop as a stitch.

Right- or left-slanting decreases (dec) (ssk)

For right slanting decreases: Insert right-hand needle into two stitches on left-hand needle, and knit these two stitches together (T12-1).

For left-slanting decreases: With right-hand needle, transfer two stitches from left-hand needle as if to knit (T13-1). Using left-hand needle, insert into fronts of transferred stitches. Wrap yarn around right-hand needle and pull through both loops.

T12-1 Insert the right-hand needle knitwise through the next two stitches on the left-hand needle. Wrap the yarn around the right-hand needle, and pull it through both loops.

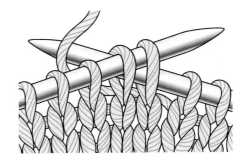

T13-1 Keeping the right-hand needle behind the left, insert through the back of the next two loops on the left-hand needle. Wrap the yarn around the right-hand needle and draw through both loops.

Center double decrease (cdd)

Pass stitches from left to right, inserting right-hand needle as if to knit both stitches together (T14-1). Knit next stitch. Using left-hand needle, pass two slipped stitches over knit stitch (T14-2).

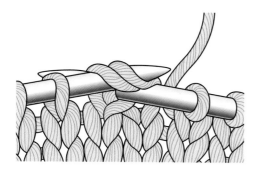

T14-1 Insert the right-hand needle knitwise and slip the next two stitches on the left over to the right-hand needle. Move a stitch from the left needle to the right needle as if to knit.

T14-2 Insert the left-hand needle into the two stitches previously slipped. Pass these two stitches over the knit stitch.

Binding off (BO)

Standard bind off

Knit two stitches. Using left-hand needle, pass stitch closest to right over the stitch to the immediate left (T15-1, T15-2).

Knit next stitch and pass right-hand stitch over (T15-3). Repeat across row as desired.

T15-1 Knit two stitches, and then insert the left needle into the first stitch on the right needle.

T15-2 Pass the first stitch on the right needle over the second.

T15-3 One stitch remains on the right-hand needle. Repeat this procedure across row.

Three-needle bind off

I love using this technique for shoulder seams or anyplace where I want a smooth joined edge. Divide stitches to be bound off in half, placing each half on its own needle. Using a third needle, knit one stitch from first needle together with one stitch from second needle (T16-1). Repeat (T16-2). Pass stitch on right over next stitch, as with a standard bind off (T16-3). Repeat across row as desired.

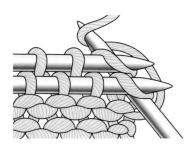

T16-1 Divide stitches to be bound off on two needles, with the points facing in the same direction. Hold the work so the right sides of garment are together.

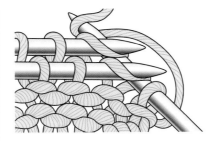

T16-2 Using a third needle, insert through the first stitch on each needle as if to knit, then draw yarn through, resulting in one loop on the right-hand needle. Repeat until there are two loops on the right-hand needle.

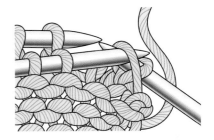

T16-3 Pass the loop on the right over the other loop as you would in a standard bind off.

Buttonholes

One-row buttonhole

Work to desired buttonhole placement, then bring working yarn to front. Slip next stitch, and bring working yarn to back. Pass first slipped stitch over the other. Repeat for desired number of stitches (T17-1). Using cable cast on method, cast on the number of stitches bound off, plus one extra (T17-2). Pass first stitch on right-hand needle over last cast on stitch, then resume working across row (T17-3).

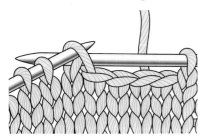

T17-1 Bind off the desired number of stitches for the buttonhole. Slip the last bound-off stitch back to the left-hand needle.

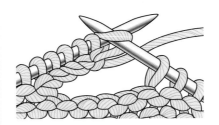

T17-2 Using the cable cast on method, cast on the number of stitches bound off, plus one extra.

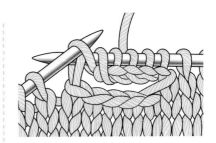

T17-3 Holding the yarn in back, slip the first stitch from the left-hand needle over to the right-hand needle; then pass the extra cast on stitch over, closing the buttonhole.

Two-row buttonhole

Bind off desired number of stitches (T18-1), work remainder of row to end. On the next row, work to bound off stitches, then using knitted cast on method, cast on the same number of stitches as were bound off (T18-2).

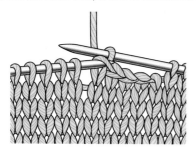

T18-1 Bind off the desired number of stitches for the buttonhole. Work to end of row.

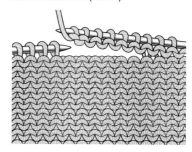

T18-2 On the following row, work across to bound off stitches; then using backward loop or knitted method, cast on the number of stitches previously bound off.

Other techniques

Knitting in the round with a circular needle

Working a piece in the round creates a tube. This method is used in the book for body bands, and leg cuffs. A few of the sweater projects in this book are worked in the round, eliminating the need to seam the garment. The needle choice is based on the number of stitches being worked. For a larger number of stitches, a circular needle is used (T19-1, T19-2).

When working a smaller number of stitches, or using a finer weight yarn, double-pointed needles are used (see sidebar on double-pointed needles, page 23). When casting on a piece to be worked in the round, join carefully to avoid twisting your work, and mark the beginning of the round. Your knitting will be worked on the right side only.

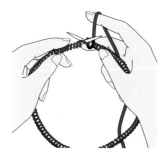

T19-1 The first cast on stitch is on the left-hand end of the circular needle, and the last is on the right-hand end. Place a marker on the right-hand needle to mark beginning of the round. Work the first stitch off the left-hand needle to join the work into the round.

T19-2 Work around to the marker: then slip the marker over to begin the next round.

Cable stitches

Adding cables is an easy way to add interest to a design. To create a cable, stitches are placed onto a small double-pointed cable needle or cable holder to be held in front or back of the work, depending on what direction the cable will move. Stitches are worked from the left-hand needle; then from the stitches held on the cable needle as the work progresses.

The right twist cable is traditionally worked as follows: Slip 3 sts onto a cable needle and leave at back of work (T20-1). Knit the next 3 sts, then knit 3 sts from cable needle (T20-2).

The left twist cable is traditionally worked as follows: Slip 3 sts onto a cable needle and leave at front of work (T20-3). Knit the next 3 sts; then knit 3 sts from cable needle. (T20-4).

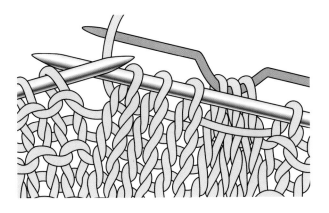

T20-1 Slip the cable stitches onto a cable or double-pointed needle, and hold to the back of the work, then knit the next stitches in the cable section.

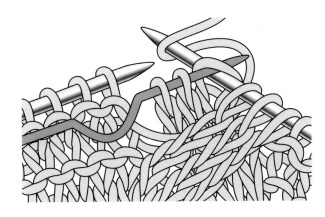

T20-2 Knit the stitches from the cable needle.

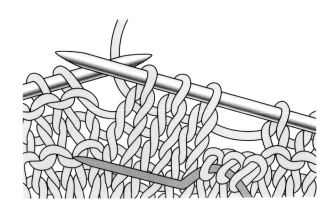

T20-3 Slip the cable stitches onto a cable or double-pointed needle, hold them to the front of the work, and then knit the next stitches in the cable section.

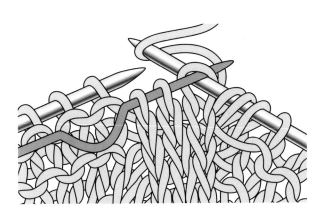

T20-4 Knit the stitches from the cable needle.

Short row shaping

Using short rows creates a three-dimensional shape that will curve around. For the patterns in this book, short rows create a curve around the hips that will help hold the sweater in place. A short row is worked by not completing a row, then wrapping a stitch with the working yarn, turning the work, and working back. After all the short rows are completed, a row is worked across all stitches, and the wraps are worked together with the live stitch to create a smooth line. Knit to the point where your pattern says to turn but don't turn the work yet (T21-1). Bring your yarn to the front of the work (T21-2). Slip the next stitch from the left-hand needle, and take your yarn to the back of the work, Slip the stitch back to the left-hand needle (T21-3). Turn your work and knit as directions specify to end. After the short rows are completed, to hide the wraps, put the needle up through the wrap on the right side of the work, put the needle through the stitch (knitways if you are going to knit the stitch, purlways if you are going to purl the stitch), and knit (or purl) the two together (T21-4).

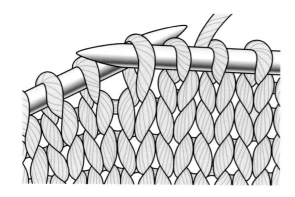

T21-1 With yarn in back, slip next stitch purlwise.

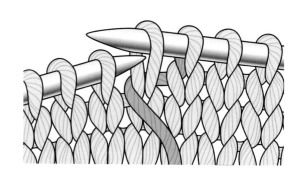

T21-2 Move the yarn between the needles to the front of the work.

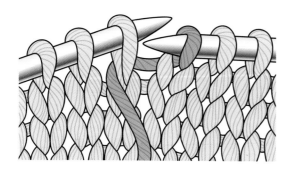

T21-3 Move the previously slipped stitch back to the left-hand needle, turn work, then work to end. Repeat as pattern directs.

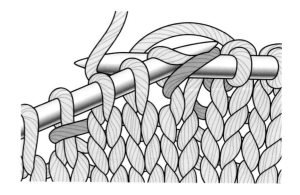

T-21-4 To hide the wraps, work to just before the wrapped stitch; then insert the right needle under the wrap and knitwise into the wrapped stitch and knit both together.

Knitting in the Round with Double-Pointed Needles

Using double-pointed needles is a method of working in the round. For double-pointed needles, your work will be distributed on three or four needles and joined in the round. Using an additional double-pointed needle, knit across each section of distributed stitches to create a tube.

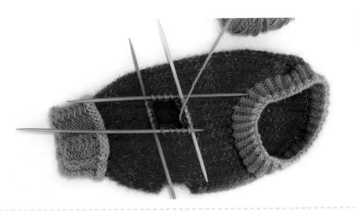

DP1.
Distribute the stitches evenly on four needles.

DP2.
Using a fifth needle, knit across the stitches that are on the first needle to your left only.

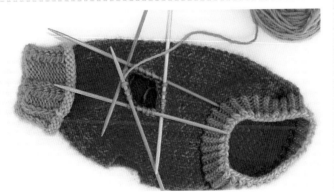

DP3.
After the stitches on the first needle are worked, the first needle is free. Use it as your new "fifth" needle.

1. Distribute the stitches evenly on four needles; here we're working on creating a leg band (Fig. DP1).

2. Using a fifth needle, work across (knit across) the stitches that are on the first needle to your left only (Fig. DP2).

3. After the stitches on the first needle are worked (knitted onto the fifth needle), the first needle is free. Use it as your new "fifth" needle (Fig. DP3). Repeat Step 2 as many times as necessary to get the number of rows you need for the leg band (or whatever you're making).

Creating Leg Holes on a Sweater Knit Flat

I prefer using a circular needle for sweaters knit flat. The advantage is that the cable serves as a holder for the stitches not being worked. Use your own comfort level with knitting to decide if you want to use circular needles. Straight needles can be used, and the stitches not being worked may be placed on holders.

LF1
Work is divided into three sections.

LF2
Beginning each section with a wrong-side row, work each section to the length specified in pattern.

1. Following pattern instructions, on right-side row, bind off the specified number of stitches in two places on row. The work will now be separated into three sections (Fig. LF1).

2. Starting on wrong side, work the first section to length specified in pattern directions, ending with a wrong-side row. Break yarn or leave a length of slack yarn to be trimmed later.

3. Starting with a wrong-side row, work the center section to length specified in pattern directions, ending with a wrong-side row (Fig. LF2). Depending on your measurements, the optional harness hole may be worked in this section. Break yarn or leave a length of slack to be trimmed later.

4. Beginning on a wrong-side row, work the last section, ending with a wrong-side row. If your sweater is knit using a self-striping yarn, work the smaller edge sections first, and the center section last, so the stripes match when the sweater is seamed.

5. After all three sections are knit, on right-side row, work across to bound off stitches, then cast on stitches as specified in pattern, using knitted cast on (Fig. LF3). Repeat as you work across row. Three sections are now joined (Fig. LF4).

LF3
On right side, cast on previously bound off stitches using knitted cast on method.

LF4
The three sections are now joined.

Creating Leg Holes on a Sweater Knit in the Round

LR1
Work is divided into two sections.

LR2
Beginning and ending with wrong-side rows, work the smaller section between leg holes to the length specified in pattern.

1. Bind off the specified number of stitches in two places on round (Fig. LR1). The work remaining on the needle is now divided into two sections (separated by two bound off sections), which will both be worked flat.

2. Starting on wrong-side row, work smaller section, between the two bound-off leg holes (Fig. LR2), to the length specified in pattern directions, ending with a wrong-side row. You may be more comfortable holding stitches not being worked on a piece of scrap yarn (Fig. LR3). Break yarn or leave a length of slack yarn to be trimmed later.

3. Tie new yarn onto the slack yarn left over from Step 2. Beginning with wrong-side row, work the larger section. Place the harness hole in this section according to your measurements, if desired. End with a wrong-side row. Turn work so right side is facing (Fig. LR4).

LR3
Hold stitches not being worked on a piece of scrap yarn.

LR4
Beginning and ending with wrong-side rows, work larger section to length specified in pattern. Use scrap yarn to hold section not being worked.

LR5
Starting on right-side row, work across larger section, casting on stitches previously bound off. Continue on to smaller section.

LR6
Work is now joined back into round.

4. On right side, work across larger section. Using knitted cast on method, cast on the number of stitches previously bound off when you get to the bound off the leg hole parts. Remove stitches of the smaller section from holder, putting them back on the needle; then work across. Cast on the number of stitches previously bound off (Fig. LR5).

5. Join work into round (Fig. LR6) and continue to work sweater as one seamless piece.

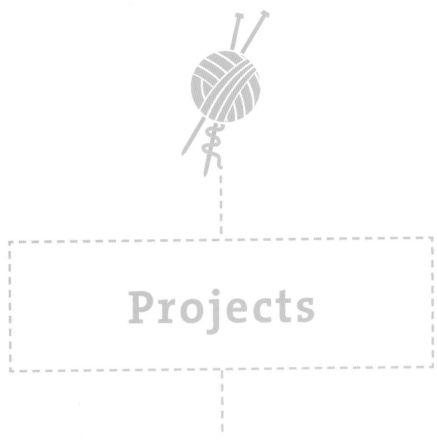

Projects

This section includes some simple projects for beginners, like the Collar Cozy and the Chickies toy. For the sweaters, a knitter should have some knowledge of shaping and garment construction. If you're a new knitter, or new to a certain technique, I suggest that you familiarize yourself with any special technique by visiting the techniques section of the book before you dive into a project. Patterns are rated by level of difficulty.

The sweaters have design details that can be transferred to another design, such as a collar or body band treatment. For an intermediate knitter, this usually involves some easy math to adapt the pattern.

For the knitter who likes a challenge, the Gidget Hoodie and Yoda sweater are two satisfying projects. The Gidget Hoodie uses the provisional cast on and three-needle bind off to assemble a little hooded garment with minimal seaming. The Yoda sweater is built from the bottom up using the domino technique made popular by Horst Schultz and Vivian Hoxbro.

Peanut, modeling a
Little Penny sweater.

LITTLE PENNY SWEATER

I intended this to be a layering piece, worn alone inside a house, or under/over a sweater for outside. The inspiration was a winter spent in a drafty apartment with two older dogs. I kept it on my little Gidget in the house when she was ill. This sweater, being ribbed, is an easy fit, and would make a good gift if you were not sure about the dog's measurements. I could see this knit in a cotton blend as a summer garment, to protect skin from sun, or to warm up in an air conditioned house. This sweater is sized for extra small (and small) dogs. Level: intermediate.

Finished size

▶ Neck: 8 to 10 (9 to 12) inches. Chest: 14 to 16 (18 to 20) inches

Materials

▶ Worsted weight yarn approximately 100 (150) yards

▶ Size 5 (3.75 mm) needles

▶ Size 6 (4 mm) circular needle, 24 inches or longer

▶ Yarn needle

Gauge

▶ 20 sts and 28 rows to 4 inches in k2 p2 rib, slightly stretched, with larger needles

DIRECTIONS

Neck

Using smaller needles, CO 46 (62) sts.

Row 1 (WS): Sl 1, p1, place marker on needle, *k2, p2*, repeat to last 2 sts, place marker on needle, p1, k1 (slip markers every row).

Row 2 (RS): Sl 1, p1, *p2, k2*, repeat to last 2 sts, p1, k1.

Repeat rows 1 and 2 until neck measures 1.5 (2) inches, ending with WS row. Change to larger (circular) needle.

Body shaping

Row 1 (RS): Sl 1, k1, m1, slip marker, work rib sts as they appear to next marker, slip marker, m1, k2.

Row 2 (WS): Sl 1, p1, k to marker, slip marker, work rib sts as they appear to next marker, k1, p1, k1.

Row 3 (RS): Sl 1, k1, m1, k to marker, slip marker, work rib sts as they appear to next marker, slip marker, k to last 2 sls, m1, k2.

Row 4 (WS): Sl 1, p1, k to marker, work rib sts as they appear to next marker, slip marker, k to last 2 sts, p1, k1.

Repeat rows 3 & 4 until you have 70 (84 sts) on needle. Work pattern as established until piece measures 4.5 (6) inches from beginning, ending with a WS row.

Divide for legs

RS: Sl 1, k6 (7), BO 5 (6) sts, work in rib as established to last 12 (14) sts, BO 5 (6) sts, k to end. Work is now divided into three sections.

Leg shaping

WS: Work each section separately, always sl first st and k last st on each section to establish/maintain selvedge. Work sts as they appear until each section measures 1.5 (1.75) inches from BO edge, ending each section on WS row. Sections not being worked are held on the cable of the circular needle.

Side view of Little Penny sweater shows leg holes and ribbing.

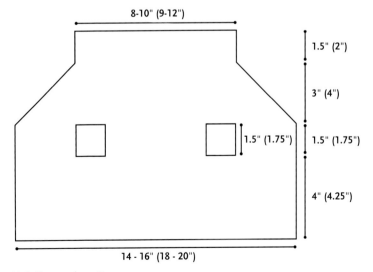

Little Penny schematic.

Body shaping

RS: Sl 1, k across first section, CO 5 (6) sts, using knitted cast on, work sts across second section as they appear, CO 5 (6) sts, k to end.

Continue to work sts as they appear until piece measures 10 (12) inches from beginning, or to desired length. BO all sts as they appear.

Finishing

Sew together left and right edges to form tube. Weave in ends.

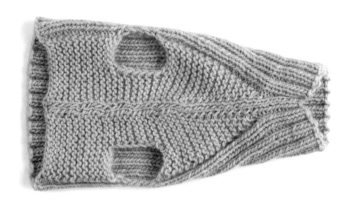

Underneath view shows spacing of leg holes and body shaping.

Woodie in a variegated Little Penny Sweater.

The ribbed body of the Little Penny sweater makes it a comfortable fit for many body shapes.

BIG PENNY SWEATER

This is the Little Penny sweater upsized to fit a larger dog. The ribbed back panel makes for an easy fit. This version incorporates additional body shaping to make a sweater that will fit the length of a bigger dog. Sized for large (and extra large) dogs. Level: intermediate.

Finished size

▶ Neck: 12 to 16 (18 to 22) inches. Chest: 17 to 28 (22 to 32) inches. Length: 26 (29) inches (excluding collar)

Materials

▶ Bulky weight yarn, approximately 220 (300) yards

▶ Size 10.5 (6.5 mm) circular needle, 32 inches or longer

Gauge

▶ 9 sts and 15 rows to 4 inches in k2 p2 rib, slightly stretched

33

DIRECTIONS

Neck

CO 46 (62) sts.

Row 1 (WS): Sl 1, p1, place marker on needle, *k2, p2*, repeat to last 2 sts, place marker on needle, p1, k1 (slip markers every row).

Row 2 (RS): Sl 1, p1, *p2, k2*, repeat to last 2 sts, p1, k1.

Repeat rows 1 and 2 until neck measures 1.5 (2) inches, ending with WS row.

Body shaping

Row 1 (RS): Sl 1, k1, m1, slip marker, work rib sts as they appear to next marker, slip marker, m1, k2.

Row 2 (WS): Sl 1, p1, k to marker, slip marker, work rib sts as they appear to next marker, k1, p1, k1.

Row 3 (RS): Sl 1, k1, m1, k to marker, slip marker, work rib sts as they appear to next marker, slip marker, k to last 2 sts, m1, k2.

Row 4 (WS): Sl 1, p1, k to marker, work rib sts as they appear to next marker, slip marker, k to last 2 sts, p1, k1.

Repeat rows 3 & 4 until you have 70 (84 sts) on needle. Work pattern as established until piece measures 4.5 (6) inches from beginning, ending with a WS row.

Divide for legs

RS: Sl 1, k6 (7), BO 5 (6) sts, work in rib as established to last 12 (14) sts, BO 5 (6) sts, k to end. Work is now divided into three sections.

Leg shaping

WS: Work each section separately; always sl first st and k last st on each section to establish/maintain selvedge. Work sts as they appear until each section measures 2 (2.5) inches from BO edge, ending each section on WS row. Sections not being worked are held on the cable of the circular needle.

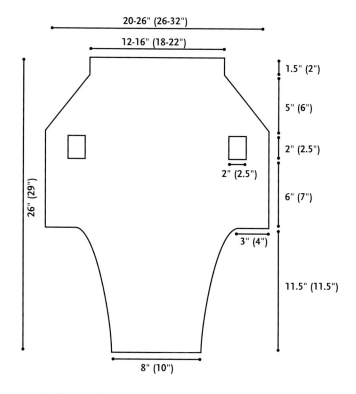

Side view of Big Penny sweater in pumpkin shows ribbing and leg hole detail.

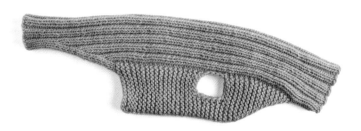

Big Penny schematic.

Body shaping

RS: S1, k across first section, CO 5 (6) sts, using knitted cast on, work sts across second section as they appear, CO 5 (6) sts, k to end. Work sts as established until 6 (7) inches from leg cast on, ending with WS row.

Decrease for lower body

BO 11 (15) sts at beginning of next two rows.

RS: Sl 1, k2, ssk, work sts as established to last 5 sts, k2tog, k to end.

WS: Sl 1, work sts as established to end.

Repeat these two rows until 28 (36) sts remain. Work sts as established until sweater is desired length, ending with WS row. BO sts on RS side as established.

Finishing

Sew center seam. Weave in ends.

Underneath view of Big Penny sweater shows leg hole placement, shaping, and stitch detail.

Skye is happy in his Big Penny sweater.

35

PICCOLO
SWEATER

This basic sweater, knit in one piece with a fold-over turtleneck with body shaping, is the jumping off point for the Lucky Penny designs. I've been making this sweater for a number of years, but have now named it after my little Piccolo because she's the ultimate chameleon. It seems like every style and color looks superb on her. This sweater can be made in a simple, basic version, or the trim, neck and body bands, and body texture can be changed in any combination to lend an entirely different look. Level: intermediate.

- Neck: 9 (10, 12, 14, 16, 18) inches. Chest: 12 (14, 16, 18, 20, 22) inches. Length: 12 (14, 16, 18, 20, 22) inches (excluding collar)

- Worsted weight yarn: Main color (MC), 90 (120, 150, 190, 250, 300) yards. Contrast color 1 (CC1), 70 (85, 100, 125, 150, 190) yards. Contrast color 2 (CC2), 15 (20, 25, 35, 45, 60) yards

- Size 5 (3.75 mm) and 6 (4.25 mm) needles, or size that will achieve gauge*

- 2 stitch holders (needed if knitting this garment with straight needles)

- Cable needle

- Size 5 (3.75 mm) circular needle, 24 to 32 inches, depending on size of dog

- Size 5 (3.75 mm) double-pointed needles, set of 5

- Yarn needle

*Note: Circular needles are recommended for holding stitches not being worked when knitting leg section of garment.

Striped Piccolo sweater on Woodie in earth tones.

Gauge

▶ 18 sts and 24 rows to 4 inches in stockinette st (k one row, p one row), using larger needles

DIRECTIONS

Turtleneck

With CC2 and smaller needles, cast on 50 (58, 66, 74, 82, 90) stitches.

Row 1 (WS): Purl.

Row 2 (RS): Sl 1, k across row. While piece is being worked, knit the last stitch on every row and slip the first stitch on every row to create selvedge.

Row 3: With CC1, sl first stitch, k across row.

Row 4: Sl 1, p1, k1, *p4, k1, p2, k1* repeat across row to last 7 sts, end p4, k1, p1, k1.

Row 5: Sl 1, work sts as established across row, end k1.

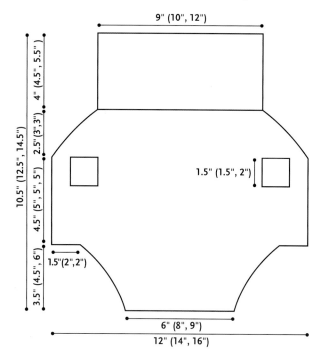

9" (10", 12")

4" (4.5", 5.5")

2.5" (3", 3")

1.5" (1.5", 2")

10.5" (12.5", 14.5")

4.5" (5", 5")

1.5"(2",2")

3.5" (4.5", 6")

6" (8", 9")

12" (14", 16")

Piccolo sweater schematic. Body band is not included in schematic.

Row 6: Sl 1, k1, p1, *sl 2 to cable needle and hold in back, k2, then k2 from cable needle, p1, k2, p1* repeat across row to last 7 sts, sl 2 to cable needle and hold in back, k2, then k2 from cable needle, p1, k2.

Row 7: Sl 1, work sts as established across row, end k1.

Row 8: Repeat row 4.

Row 9: Repeat row 7.

Repeat rows 4 through 9 for 4 (5.5, 6) inches, ending with RS row. Break yarn.

Body

With MC yarn, sl 1, k across. At this point, the right side of the sweater reverses, and the wrong side of the turtleneck will be on the right side of the body.

Row 1 (RS): Sl 1, k across.

Row 2 (WS): Sl 1, p to last st, k1.

Row 3: Sl 1, k1, m1, k to last 2 sts, m1, k2.

Row 4: Repeat row 2.

Repeat rows 3 and 4 four (5, 5, 6, 6, 5) more times, for a total of 60 (70, 78, 86, 96, 102) sts. Continue in stockinette st, maintaining selvedges, for 2.5 (3, 3.5, 4, 4.5, 4.5) inches, ending with WS row.

Leg openings

RS: Sl 1, k6 (8, 9, 12, 12, 14), BO next 5 (6, 6, 7, 7, 8) sts, k to last 12 (14, 15, 20, 20, 23) sts, BO 5 (6, 6, 7, 7, 8) sts, k to end. Work is now divided into three sections. Work each section separately, slipping first stitch and knitting last stitch on every row to maintain selvedge, for 1.5 (1.5, 2, 2, 2.25, 2.25) inches, ending with WS row. Use stitch holders for unworked sections if knitting on straight needles.

Close leg openings

Sl 1, k6 (8, 9, 12, 12, 14), CO 5 (6, 6, 7, 7, 8) sts, k across middle section, CO 5 (6, 6, 7, 7, 8) sts, k to end.

Continue knitting in stockinette st, maintaining selvedges, until work measures 7 (8, 8.5, 9, 9.5 10) inches from beginning of body.

Body shaping

BO 7 (9, 10, 12, 12, 14) sts at beginning of next two rows.

Striped Piccolo
sweater on Lyubi.

Underneath view of finished Piccolo sweater.

Side view of the finished Piccolo sweater.

Decrease rows

RS: Sl 1, k1, ssk, k to last 4 sts, k2tog, k2.
WS: For all WS rows, continue stockinette, maintaining the selvedges, without shaping.

Repeat the RS decrease row 6 (7, 8, 9, 13, 13) more times, until 30 (36, 40, 42, 44, 46) sts remain.
Work stockinette st, maintaining selvedges, until body measures 10.5 (12.5, 14.5, 16.5, 18.5, 20.5) inches, or 1.5 inches less than desired finished length, ending with a WS row.

Short-row shaping

RS: K to last 3 sts, wrap and turn, p to last 3 sts, wrap and turn, k to last 6 sts, wrap and turn, p to last 6 sts, wrap and turn. Move last unworked sts to right-hand needle. Break yarn.

Sew together turtleneck and body, creating a tube.

39

Body band

With smaller needles and CC1, k across 30 (36, 40, 42, 44, 46) sts on body, knitting up wraps as they appear. Pick up 36 (46, 52, 60, 70, 80) sts on edge of sweater, for a total 66 (82, 92, 102, 114, 126) sts.

Work 5 rounds in k1, p1 rib. Break yarn.
With CC2, k one round. Work 1 round k1, p1 rib as established. BO in rib.

Leg bands

With dp needles and CC1, pick up 5 (5, 6, 7, 7, 8) sts on each of 4 sides of leg for 20 (20, 24, 28, 28, 32) sts. Work 5 rounds of k1, p1, rib. Break yarn. With CC2, k one round. Work 1 round k1, p1 rib as established. BO in rib.

Finishing

Weave in ends. Steam lightly if needed.

Teddy in a variegated Piccolo sweater. Cranberry tone in body is picked up for leg bands.

Kinsey the Chinese Crested in a Piccolo variation sweater with eyelet trim, twist cable collar, and waffle stitch body.

PICCOLO VARIATIONS

Changing one or more of the elements of the basic Piccolo sweater gives you endless possibilities for customization. Below are some favorites.

Edge variations

EYELET
Use long-tail cast on.
RS: Yo, p2tog across row, end k1 for selvedge.
WS: Sl 1, k across row.

EYELET WITH FRINGE
Cut yarn into 3-inch lengths. Using a crochet hook, hang 2 strands together in each eyelet, and tie them in a knot. Trim fringe to desired length.

Varying bands in collar

ROPE CABLE
Use a multiple of 8 sts plus 2.
Row 1 (WS): Sl 1, k2, *p4, k4*; repeat across work to last 7 sts, end p4, k3.
Row 2 (RS): Sl 1, p2, *k2tog, leave on left-hand needle, k in first st, move both sts to right-hand needle, ktbl of 2nd st on left-hand needle, k in first st on left-hand needle, move both sts to right-hand needle, p4*; repeat to last 3 stitches, p2, k1.

TWIST CABLE
This stitch pattern uses a multiple of 10 stitches plus 2. You may need to adjust the increases on the body shaping to compensate for any difference in stitch count on the collar.

Twist cable collar.

Rope cable collar with fringe trim, detail.

Row 1 (WS): Sl 1, k2, *p6, k4*; repeat across work to last 9 sts, end p6, k3.

Row 2 (RS): Sl 1, p2, *(k2tog, leave on left-hand needle, k first st, move both to the right-hand needle), 3 times, p4* across work, end p2, k1.

Row 3: Repeat row 1.

Row 4: Sl 1, p2, *k1, (k2 tog, leave on left-hand needle, k first st, move both to the right-hand needle) twice, k1, p4*, repeat from *across work, end p2, k1.

Repeat these four rows for pattern.

SIMPLE BAND

Use a multiple of 2 or 4 sts.

For a collar made from a mohair, boucle, or highly textured yarn, a simple k1, p1 or k2, p2 ribbing works best.

GARTER STITCH COLLAR

Slipping first st of row, k every row until half of desired length, then switch to k1, p1 or k2, p2 ribbing for the remainder of collar.

Romeo Princeton in Piccolo variation sweater with contrasting cuffs and body band, and rope cable collar with fringe trim.

Side view of fringed Piccolo sweater shows rope cable collar, with fringe trim, leg bands, and body band shaping.

Piccolo variation with rope cable collar and garter stitch body in lavender tones.

Body variations

WAFFLE BODY

This is my favorite stitch pattern for surface interest on dog sweaters. It reminds me of the texture of thermal underwear. Try a swatch in your intended yarn to see the texture. I have found that the texture does not look good in all yarns.

Row 1 (WS): p.

Row 2 (RS): K1tbl, p1 across work.

GARTER STITCH BODY

Knitting every row will also lend an interesting texture to the sweater; however, it will alter the row gauge, so allow for extra yarn when choosing materials for your sweater.

Band variations*

TWISTED RIB

Use a multiple of 2 sts. K1tbl, p1 for every round.

GARTER BANDS

K one round, p one round. For body bands, k2tog at each lower corner of body, every knit round.

*Note: Eliminating the leg bands is a good idea for a dog with short legs or those that may have a tendency to squirm out of the sweater.

Mr. Lucky sports a green Piccolo variation sweater.

Woodie models a striped Piccolo variation sweater. A simple k2, p2 rib is used for the fluffy mohair collar.

Zoey in a turquoise Agnes sweater.

AGNES SWEATER

This little sweater was born out of necessity. A potential new member of the family does not like tight things pulled over her head, so the solution is a paper bag type neck, closed with a drawstring. Mostly knit in the round from the top down, there is a little bit of flat knitting for creating the leg holes and for the lower body shaping. Level: intermediate.

Finished size

▶ Chest: 12 (14, 16) inches. Length: 12 (14, 16) inches (excluding collar)

Materials

▶ Worsted weight yarn: Main color (MC), 90 (120, 150) yards. Contrast color 1 (CC1), 70 (85, 100) yards. Contrast color 2 (CC2), 15 (18, 25) yards

▶ Size 6 (4 mm) circular needle, 16 inches long

▶ Size 5 (3.75 mm) circular needle, 16 inches long

▶ Size 5 (3.75 mm) double-pointed needles, set of 5

▶ Yarn needle

Gauge

▶ 18 sts and 26 rows to 4 inches using larger needle

DIRECTIONS

With CC2, cast on 56 (64, 72) sts. Join into the round, place marker at beginning of round. Work k2, p2 ribbing for 2 rounds. Change to CC1, k every st for one round; then resume k2, p2 ribbing as established for 3 (3.5, 3.5) inches.

For eyelet round: K2, *p2 tog, yo, k2, yo, p2 tog, k2*, repeat to end of round, end p2tog. K every st next round, change to MC, and continue in stockinette stitch (k every round) until sweater measures 6 inches from beginning.

Leghole shaping

K6 (7, 8), BO 5 (6, 6), k to last 11 (13, 14) sts before marker, BO 5 (6, 6), k to marker. Work is now divided into two sections.

Note: keeping work on circ needle, attach second ball of yarn and work in flat rows (back and forth) across both sections every row, continuing in stockinette st (k 1 row, p 1 row) throughout leghole shaping. Keep marker in place (slip marker every row).

Work until each section is 1 (1.5, 1.5) inch above bound-off sts. If a harness hole is desired, work your preferred buttonhole into the back section. End on a WS (p) row. To complete leghole shaping, join work back into round by casting on 5 (6, 6) stitches where previously bound off in next round. You will again have 56 (64,72 sts) on needle.

Continue to work in the round for 2 (2.5, 3) inches after leghole cast on.

Body shaping

Continuing in stockinette st, work next round to 8 (10, 10) sts before marker, BO 8 (10, 10) stitches, remove marker, BO 8 (10, 10) stitches, k1, ssk, k to last 4 stitches, k2tog, k2. You will have 38 (42, 50) sts on needle.

Note: for remainder of sweater you will be working in flat rows, back and forth on circ needle in stockinette st.

Next row (WS): Sl 1, p across.

RS: Sl 1, k1, ssk, k to last 4 sts, k2 tog, k2.

Repeat these two rows until 28 (30, 32) sts remain. Continue in stockinette st until sweater is 1.5 inches less than the desired final length, end with WS (p) row.

Bee in an Agnes sweater with stripes of warm pinks, purples, and oranges.

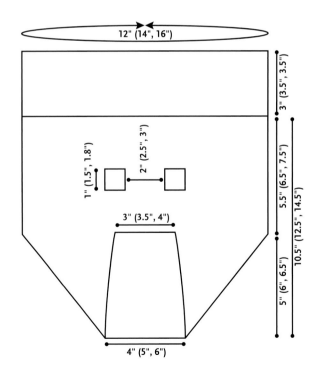

Schematic for Agnes sweater; does not include body band.

Short row shaping

RS: K to last 3 sts, wrap and turn, p to last 3 sts, wrap and turn, k to last 6 sts, wrap and turn, p to last 6 sts, wrap and turn. Move last unworked sts to right-hand needle. Break yarn.

Body band

With smaller needles and CC1, k across 28 (30, 32) sts on body, knitting up wraps as they appear; pick up 36 (46, 52) sts on edge of sweater for a total 66 (82, 92) sts. Work 5 rounds in k1, p1 rib. Break yarn. With CC2, k one round. Work 1 round in k1, p1 rib as established. BO in rib.

Leg bands

With dp needles and CC1, pick up 5 (5, 6) sts on each of 4 sides of leg for 20 (20, 24) sts. Work 5 rounds in k1, p1, rib. Break yarn. With CC2, k one round. Work 1 round in k1, p1 rib as established. BO in rib.

To finish

Weave in ends and block if desired.

To make drawstring: Knit 24 (26, 28) inches of I-cord. Weav ends, thread it through drawstring sweater eyelets.

The gathered neck treatment makes the sweater easy to put on a squirmy puppy.

View of whole Agnes sweater from underneath.

ZeeNa in an Agnes sweater featuring purple, blue and earth tone stripes.

Lyubi in a Gidget sweater; note kangaroo pocket on sweater back.

GIDGET HOODIE SWEATER

This is the very sweater I would have loved to bundle my little Gidget in, to keep her cozy for a snooze after a bath, or in the pet carrier on the way to the vet. This comfy sweater is fashioned after your favorite sweatshirt, combining some advanced knitting techniques. It is worked from the top down from a provisional cast on. A hood, knit as a separate piece, is later attached using a three-needle bind off. Buttonholes are placed while the body is knit, so read through entire instructions before beginning. Optional details include a buttonhole at the neck for a collar, and mid-back buttonhole for a harness. The result will be a sweater needing minimal finishing, apart from weaving in ends and sewing on buttons. Self-striping yarns work very well with the top-down design. For the Hollywood dog, a fluffy cashmere blend is a fashion-forward choice. Level: advanced.

Finished size

▶ Neck: 12 (14, 16, 18, 21) inches. Chest: 16 (19, 20, 24, 26) inches. Length (without hood): 12 (14, 16, 18, 20) inches

47

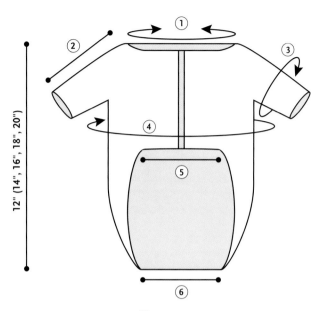

12" (14", 16", 18", 20")

Key
1. 12" (14", 16", 18", 21")
2. 6" (6", 6", 8", 8.5")
3. 5" (6", 6.5", 8", 10")
4. 16" (19", 20", 24", 26")
5. 5" (5.5", 6", 8", 9")
6. 4.5" (5", 5.5", 6", 7.5")

Gidget sweater schematic; body band is not included.

Materials

- Worsted weight wool yarn, 180 (250, 300, 375, 450) yards, depending on dog's size

- 5/8-inch buttons, 5

- Size 6 (4 mm) needles, straight or circular

- Size 6 (4 mm) double-pointed needles, 1 set

- Size 5 (3.75 mm) circular needle, 24 to 32 inches long

- Size 5 (3.75 mm) double-pointed needles, 1 set

- Waste yarn for provisional cast on

- Crochet hook size H (5.0 mm)

- Stitch holders, 2

- Stitch markers, 4

- Yarn needle

Gauge

- 18 stitches and 24 rows to 4 inches in stockinette stitch, with larger size needles

Lyubi in a Gidget sweater, front view showing button band detail.

DIRECTIONS

Body

Using crochet hook, chain 60 (70, 80, 90, 100) with waste yarn. Mark end of chain with knot. This knot will be used later to identify the end from which start to easily remove stitches. Cast on 48 (56, 66, 76, 88) in chain bumps (the loops on the wrong side of the crochet chain).

Row 1 (WS): K1, *p1, k1*, repeat once, p 38 (46, 56, 66, 78), k1, *p1, k1*, repeat once.

Row 2 (RS): K1, *p1, k1*, repeat once, k3 (4, 5, 6, 7), pm, k9 (11, 13, 15, 18), pm, k14 (16, 20, 24, 28), pm, k9 (11, 13, 15, 18), pm, k4 (5, 6, 7, 8), *p1, k1*, repeat once.

Row 3: Repeat row 1, slipping markers every row.

These three rows establish a moss stitch border on first and last 5 stitches, which will continue until body shaping decreases.

Raglan increases

Row 4: *Work stitches as established to 1 st before marker, m1, k1, slip marker, k1, m1,* repeat at each marker across row, to last 5 sts, work moss st as established.

Row 5: Maintaining moss st borders, p across, slipping markers. Repeat rows 4 and 5 three (4, 4, 4, 5) times for 80 (96, 106, 116, 136) sts. Then repeat increases on every other RS row (every 4th row) 2 (2, 3, 3, 3) times for 96 (112, 130, 140, 160) sts.

Work sts as established until sweater measures 3 (3.5, 4, 4.5, 5) inches, ending with WS row.

Create sleeve openings

RS: K to marker, remove marker, k2, place next 19 (23, 25, 27, 32) sts on holder, cast on 6 (8, 10, 12, 14) sts, k2, remove marker, k to next marker, remove marker, k2, place next 19 (21, 25, 27, 32) sts on holder, cast on 6 (8, 10, 12, 14), k2, remove marker, work remaining sts as established to end for 72 (82, 100, 110, 124) sts. Work sts as established until sweater measures 5.5 (8, 9.5, 10, 10.5) inches.

Buttonholes

Beginning with row 4, and as sweater is being worked, place buttonholes 1 (2, 2, 2, 2.5) inches apart. On right side, work sts as established to last 4 sts, BO 2 sts, work to end. On following row, work 2 sts, cast on 2, work sts as established to end. (If you'd rather use a snap placket, see design modifications below.)

Optional harness hole

When garment measures 5 inches from beginning (to assure proper placement, measure your dog wearing harness) make 4-stitch buttonhole in center using preferred method.

Body shaping

Bind off 10 (12, 15, 18, 21) sts at beginning of next 2 rows.

Bind off 2 sts at beginning of next 4 rows until 44 (50, 62, 66, 74 sts) remain.

Work decreases on every RS row as follows: Sl 1, k1, ssk, k to last 4 sts, k2tog, k2.

On WS, sl 1, p to end. Slipping sts at beginning of row will establish a selvedge edge, which will make picking up stitches for the body band easier.

Repeat until 30 (32, 36, 42, 46) sts remain. Work additional rows if needed, until sweater length is 2 inches less than desired final length.

Whole Gidget sweater seen from underneath shows buttons and body band arrangement.

Short row shaping

RS: Sl 1, k to last 2 sts, wrap and turn (2 sts on left-hand needle).
WS: Sl 1, p to last 2 sts, wrap and turn (2 sts on right-hand needle).
RS: Sl 1, k to last 4 sts, wrap and turn (4 sts on left-hand needle).
WS: Sl 1, p to last 4 sts, wrap and turn. Place all stitches on holder.

Sleeves

Divide sts on one sleeve opening holder to 2 dpns. Along cast-on edge of sleeve opening, use third dpn to pick up 7 (9, 11, 13, 14) sts for a total of 26 (32, 36, 40, 46) sts.
Working in rounds on dp needles, knit every round (stockinette st) for 1 (1, 1, 1.5, 2) inch. Changing to smaller dpns, k1, p1 for 1 inch. Bind off in rib. Repeat for 2nd sleeve.

Pocket

Crochet chain 30 (30, 40, 40, 50) sts with waste yarn, mark end with knot.
Cast on 20 (22, 24, 30, 34) sts in chain loops.
P one row. Work 5 rows moss st, ending on RS row.
Continuing to work first and last 4 sts in moss pattern, use stockinette for 2 (2, 3, 4, 5) inches, ending with WS row.
Work moss st on entire pocket for 5 rows. Bind off in knit.
Unravel crochet chain, placing live stitches on holder.

Body band

The body band is the ribbed edging around the body opening.
With RS facing, pick up 30 (32, 33, 42, 51) sts along first shaped edge from one front corner of sweater to holder, k5 (5, 6, 6, 6) from holder, knit next 20 (22, 24, 28, 34) sts together with 20 (22, 24, 30, 34) sts from pocket holder (attaching pocket to body), k5 (5, 6, 6, 6) from holder, pick up 30 (32, 33, 42, 51) sts along next shaped edge to front corner for a total of 90 (96, 102, 126, 148) sts.
Next row (WS): K1, p1 across.
Maintaining first and last 5 sts in moss pattern, continue k1, p1 ribbing for 1 inch, ending with WS row. Place buttonhole on row 2 of band. Bind off as established.

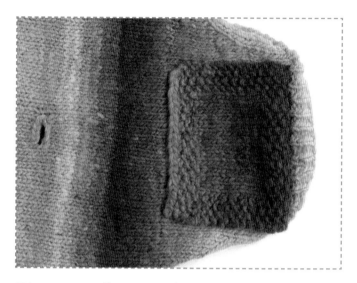

Gidget sweater in self-striping yarn; closeup shows moss stitch on pocket.

Chico in a striped Gidget sweater.

Pastel cashmere yarn was used for these Gidget sweaters.

Hood

Crochet chain 50 (60, 70, 80, 90) sts with waste yarn, tie knot to mark end of chain.

Cast on 38 (46, 56, 66, 78) sts in chain loops.

Row 1 (WS): K1, *p1, k1*, repeat once, p28 (36, 46, 56, 68), k1, *p1, k1*, repeat once.

Row 2 (RS): K1, *p1, k1*, repeat once, k29 (37, 47, 57, 67), *p1, k1*, repeat once.

Repeat these two rows until hood measures 4.5 (5.5, 6, 7, 8) inches.

Divide for top

Place 19 (23, 28, 33, 39) sts on each of 2 double-pointed needles. Placing right sides together, bind off using three-needle method. (Refer to techniques chapter for 3-needle bind-off if needed.)

Attaching hood to body

Mark center 4 stitches of both body and hood edge, if a button-hole is desired. Unravel chain cast on for each, placing live stitches on separate circular needles. Bind off first 5 button band stitches. (The button band is the edge at each side.) With right sides of body and hood together, using three-needle bind off, work across to marked center stitches. Bind off four stitches on one side of either hood or body. Break off yarn. Reattaching yarn, bind off unworked center 4 stitches, then resume three-needle bind off to last 5 sts, then continue bind off.

Finishing

Weave in ends. Wash and block to measurements. Attach top of pocket to body of sweater, leaving sides open. Sew on buttons.

Design modifications

1. Substitute snap tape for buttons, eliminating buttonholes. Using grosgrain ribbon, make your own custom snap tape.

2. Work pocket entirely in moss stitch.

3. Sew sides of pocket to sweater, leaving top open, for a functional pocket.

4. Use cashmere yarn for a luxurious look.

Woodie in a lavender Gidget sweater.

Rear view of Woodie in the Gidget sweater shows pocket and hood.

SHADOW SWEATER

From one direction, this is a striped sweater. Looking at it from another direction, it's checked. This is the beauty of shadow knitting. For a dog sweater, it creates a holographic effect that changes as your dog moves. Only one color is worked at a time, and the right side is always knit. Alternating knitting and purling on the wrong side of the work creates the illusion. For the best effect, use a very dark color for the background (main color). Level: intermediate.

Materials

▸ Worsted weight yarn: Main color (MC), 90 (120, 150, 180) yards. Each of 5 highly contrasting colors (CC1 through CC5): 20 (30, 40, 50, 60) yards

▸ Size 5 (3.75 mm) and 6 (4 mm) needles or to obtain gauge

▸ Size 5 (3.75 mm) circular needle, 24 inches long

▸ Size 5 (3.75 mm) double-pointed needles, set of 5

▸ Stitch holders (if using straight needles), 2

▸ Yarn needle

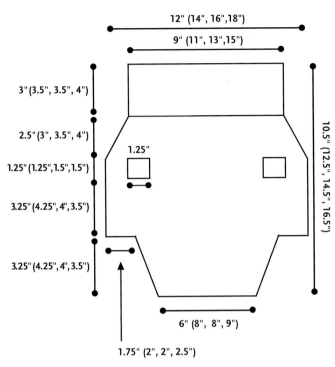

Shadow schematic. Body band is not included in schematic.

Gauge

▸ 18 sts and 34 rows to 4 inches in shadow pattern

Finished size

▸ Neck: 9 (11, 13, 15) inches. Chest: 12 (14, 16, 18) inches. Finished length: 12 (14, 16, 18) inches (excluding collar)

DIRECTIONS

Collar

With CC1, cast on 42 (50, 58, 64) sts. Slipping first st and knitting last st of every row, work in k2, p2 ribbing for 3 rows, break yarn. RS: with MC, knit across row. Continuing with MC, work in k2, p2 ribbing as previously established until work measures

3 (3.5, 4) inches from beginning, ending with a RS row. At this point in the work, the wrong side of the collar becomes the right side of the body of the sweater; later the collar will be folded over and its right side will end up outwards.

Body shaping/Begin Shadow stitch

Note: Change colors every 2 rows as indicated on Shadow St chart.

Row 1 (RS): Sl 1, k across, increasing 0 (2, 4, 6) sts evenly spaced across row for 42 (52, 62, 72) sts.

Row 2 (WS): Sl 1, place marker on needle, *Shadow St row 2 pattern*, repeat to last st, place marker on needle, k1. Slip markers every row.

Row 3: Sl 1, m1, k across, slip marker, m1, k1.

Row 4: Sl 1, p to marker, *Shadow St row 4 pattern*, repeat to marker, p to last st, end k1.

(ctd. on p. 54)

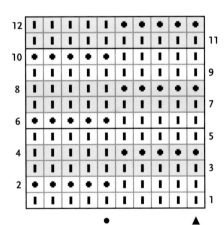

Shadow chart, showing knitting pattern for several sizes.

Key

Odd-numbered (RS) rows: follow chart R to L

Even-numbered (WS) rows: follow chart L to R

▲ Start Shadow St pattern rows here on Row 1 after completing collar

● Start rows from here after adding 5 sts on either side of row

☐ MC

▨ CC

I K on RS rows, P on WS rows

+ K on RS rows and WS rows

Row 5: Repeat row 3.

Row 6: Sl 1, p to marker, *Shadow St pattern for corresponding row*, repeat to marker, p to last st, end k1.

Rows 7 through 12: Repeat rows 5 and 6.

Reposition markers: You now have enough sts added each side for another Shadow St repeat. Move each marker 5 sts out toward beginning and end of row. Note: This will change where you begin the Shadow St repeat, by 5 sts. Follow the Shadow St pat chart starting each row at the center mark (6th stitch) then repeating across the full 10 stitches of the pattern, for the next 12 rows.

Continue to work in Shadow St as established and increase every RS row until you have 56 (66, 74, 84) sts. Continue working in shadow pattern, changing contrast color every 12 rows, until work measures 2.5 (3, 3.5, 4) inches or desired depth from beginning of body, ending with WS row.

Shadow sweater, seen from underneath.

Side view of Shadow sweater.

Leg shaping

RS: Sl 1, work 6 (8, 9, 10) sts in pattern, BO 5 (5, 6, 6) sts, work across row to last 12 (13, 15, 17) sts, BO 5 (5, 6, 6) sts, work to end. Work is divided into three sections.

Work each section separately, maintaining shadow pattern, for 1.25 (1.25, 1.5, 1.5) inches, ending with WS row on each section.

On next RS row, k across sts as established, CO 5 (5, 6, 6) sts, k across sts as established, CO 5 (5, 6, 6) sts, k to end. Continue the shadow pattern until sweater body measures 7 (8.5, 9, 10) inches from beginning.

Lower body shaping

On next two rows, BO 8 (9, 10, 12) sts.

RS: Sl 1, k1, ssk, k to last 4 sts, k2tog, k1.

WS: Continue to work shadow pattern as established.

Repeat these two rows until 28 (36, 38, 40) sts remain. Continue to knit in pattern as established until sweater is 1.25 inches less than desired finished length. Place sts on holder.

Sew center seam of sweater closed with yarn.

Body band

Using circular needle, with MC, k across 28 (36, 38, 40) sts from body, pick up 46 (54, 64, 70) from lower edge of sweater for 74 (90, 102, 110) sts. Work k1, p1 ribbing for 5 rows; break yarn. With CC3, k one round, then work 1 round in ribbing as established. Bind off in rib.

Leg bands

With four double-pointed needles and MC, pick up 5 (5, 6, 6) sts around each edge of leg opening for total 20 (20, 24, 24) sts. Work in k1, p1 rib for 5 rounds, break yarn. With CC2 for one leg and CC5 for one leg, k one round. Work 1 round in ribbing as established. Bind off in rib.

Finishing

Weave in ends and block if desired.

Penny (left) and Co-pilot in Lemon sweaters.

LEMON SWEATER

A thick neck, full chest, and then it stops short—that's the Pug figure. When I've made sweaters for Pugs, they almost look distorted. This sweater is named for one of the Pugs that wears one, Lemon, a little girl who lives in Chicago. It uses design features that make a Lucky Penny sweater. The turtleneck is cabled, the body has a broken twisted rib that reminds me of thermal underwear, and it has color changes at the edges to spark things up. Level: intermediate.

Materials

- Worsted weight yarn: Main color (MC) 175 (200, 250) yards. Contrast color 1 (CC1), 80 (90, 100) yards. Contrast color 2 (CC2), 25 (30, 40) yards

- Size 5 (3.75 mm) and 6 (4.25 mm) circular needles, 24 or 32 inches long, as needed

- Size 5 (3.75 mm) double-pointed needles, set of 5

- Stitch holders (if you use straight needles for project), 2

- Yarn needle

Finished size

▸ Neck: 10 (14, 16) inches. Chest: 16 (20, 24) inches.
Length: 11 (13, 15) inches (excluding collar)

Gauge

▸ 18 sts and 24 rows to 4 inches in stockinette stitch, using
larger needles

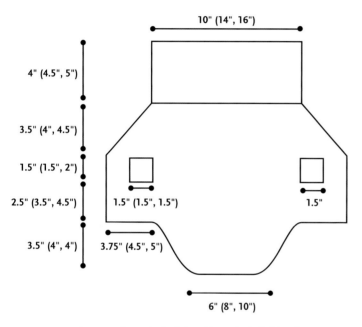

Lemon schematic. Body band is not included in schematic.

DIRECTIONS

Note: Maintain selvedge edge on each side by knitting last
stitch on every row and slipping first stitch on every row.

Collar

With CC2, using long-tail method, cast on 58 (74, 82) stitches.
P one row. K next row.
Changing to CC1, k across row, which now establishes right side.

Cable setup for collar

Row 1 (WS): Sl 1, k1, *p6, k2*, repeat to end.
Row 2 (RS): Sl 1, p1, *sl 2 sts to cable needle, hold in back of work,
k1, k sts on cable needle. Sl next st on cable needle, hold in front
of work, k2, k st on cable needle, p2*. Repeat from * until 2 sts
remain, p1, k1.
Row 3: Repeat row 1.
Row 4: Sl 1, p1, *k6, p2*, repeat until 2 sts remain, p1, k1.
Repeat rows 1 through 4 until collar measures 4 (4.5, 4.5) inches
from beginning, ending with a RS row.
Optional collar hole: On last row, bind off 4 center sts. On next
row, cast on 4 sts in center using knitted cast on.

Body

With WS of collar facing, k across, casting on 4 stitches in center
if collar hole has been worked. P next row. Maintain selvedge on
edges as established.

Begin broken twisted rib

RS: Sl 1, *k1tbl, p1*, repeat across work to last st, end k1.
WS: Sl 1, p across to last st, end k1.
Increase 1 st on each end of RS row 11 (10, 9) times for 80 (94,
100) sts.
Continue to work in pattern as established until work measures
3.5 (4, 4.5) inches from beginning of body, ending with WS row.

Leg shaping

RS: Work 10 (12, 13) sts in pattern, bind off 6 (6, 7) sts, work to last
16 (18, 20) sts, bind off 6 (6, 7) sts, work in pattern to end. Work
is now divided into three sections.
Maintaining selvedges by slipping first stitch and knitting last
stitch of every row for each section, continuing in rib pattern as
established, work each section for 1.5 (1.5, 2) inches, ending with
a WS row. Work a buttonhole in center section if desired for
harness.
RS: Working across each section in rib pattern as established,
cast on 6 (6, 7) sts over openings to complete leg holes. Continue
to work in stitch pattern for 2.5 (3.5, 4.5) inches after leg shaping, ending with WS row.

Body shaping

RS: Bind off 17 (21, 23) at beginning of next two rows.

On next RS row, sl 1, k1, ssk, work to last 4 sts, k2 tog, k2.

On following WS row, sl 1, p to last st, k1.

Repeat these two rows for a total of 4 (7, 7) increase rows until 38 (38, 40) sts remain. Work sts as established on the two pattern rows until body is 1.5 inches less than desired finished length, ending with WS row.

Short-row shaping

RS: Work to last 5 sts, wrap and turn, work to last 5 sts, placing unworked sts on right-hand needle. Place all remaining sts on holder. These live stitches will later be used in the body band. Sew center front of sweater together.

Body band

Using smaller size circular needle and CC1, k38 (38, 40) sts from holder, knitting up wraps as they appear, and pick up 42 (54, 60) evenly spaced around remainder of edge for 80 (92, 100) sts. Work 5 rows of ktbl, p1 ribbing in rounds (first rnd: *ktbl, p1*, repeat to end, 2nd rnd: k all sts).

Detail of sweater shows collar pattern.

Changing to CC2, ktbl, k1 for one round, then work ktbl, p1 as previously established in the main color. Bind off in rib.

Leg bands

Using 4 double-pointed needles and CC1, pick up 6 (6, 7) sts on each side of leg hole for 24 (24, 28) sts. Working in rounds, complete as for body band.

To finish

Weave in ends. Block or steam as desired.

The completed Lemon sweater, side view.

The completed Lemon sweater, viewed from underneath.

Zoey models an Astro sweater.

ASTRO SWEATER

I received an order for a custom sweater that posed a challenge. Astro was a one-pound Chihuahua puppy and was yet to be received by his mom. The only measurement I had was his weight. I originally used a purchased sweater, the tiniest size I could find, for the template. Another challenge was that his mom wanted a machine-washable yarn. I normally have a bias against machine-washable wool for dog sweaters, but in this case, I thought that sock yarn would be ideal. The weight would be just right for a tiny dog, and what could be more durable than sock yarn, when you think about what a beating hand knit socks take? Some tricky bits to this sweater are turning the work so the wrong side of the turtleneck becomes the right side of the body, and switching from circular to straight knitting for some body shaping. The yardage for the contrasting colors is so little that leftovers from knitting socks could be enough. Don't let the small size fool you; there is a lot of knitting here, but if you can knit socks, this project should not be difficult. Level: intermediate.

Finished size

▶ Neck: 7.5 (8.5, 9.5) inches. Chest: 9.5 (10.75, 12.5) inches. Length: 6 (7, 8) inches (excluding collar)

Materials

▶ Fingering weight yarn. Main color (MC), 175 (200, 230) yards. Contrast color 1 (CC1), 90 (105, 120) yards. Contrast color 2 (CC2), 40 (45, 50) yards

▶ Size 1 (2.25 mm) and 2 (2.75 mm) double-pointed needles, 1 set of each size

▶ Size 1 (2.25 mm) circular needle, 16 inches long, or size to obtain gauge, if desired for body band (or use double-pointed needles)

▶ Stitch holder

▶ Yarn needle

Gauge

▶ 15 sts and 20 rows to 2 inches on size 2 needles

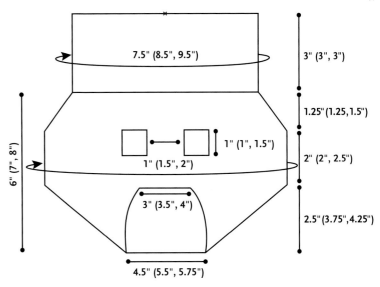

Astro schematic. Body band is not included in schematic.

DIRECTIONS

Collar

With larger size double-pointed needles and CC2 yarn, cast on 57 (65, 73) sts, join sts to work in the round. Place marker to indicate beginning of round. As you p the first round, switch to smaller size double-pointed needles. P one more round. Change to CC1 and k one round. (See directions for working on double-pointed needles in the Techniques part of the book if needed.)

HOW TO DO TWIST PATTERN FOR COLLAR

Right twist: K2 together, leaving sts on left-hand needle. K into first st on left-hand needle, slip both to right needle.

Left twist: K2 together, leaving sts on left-hand needle. K into back loop of second sts on left-hand needle, slip both to right needle.

CABLE SETUP ON COLLAR

Round 1: K1, p2, *k4, p4*, repeat until 6 sts remain, end k4 p2.

Round 2: K1, p2, *right twist, left twist, p4*, repeat until 6 sts remain, end right twist, left twist, p2.

Repeat these two rounds until work measures 3 (3, 3) inches. Turn work inside out. Transfer last st on right-hand needle to left-hand needle, making it first st on round.

Changing to MC, k one round. Reposition marker to indicate new beginning of round.

Body increases

Round 1: K1, m1, k to end of round, m1.

Round 2: K.

Repeat these two rounds 6 (7, 9) more times for 71 (81, 93) sts.

Leghole shaping

K8 (9, 10), bind off 7 (8, 9), k to last 14 (16, 18) sts, bind off 7 (8, 9), then k next 7 (8, 9), k8 (9, 10) sts from beginning of round, ending at first set of bound-off sts, turn work. Work is now divided into 2 sections. Work back and forth on this narrower section of 15 (17, 19) sts between the two leg openings. Remove marker.

Next row: Sl 1, p across to last st, end k1. These 15 (17, 19) sts will now be worked back and forth, slipping first st and knitting last st each row to create selvedge. Place remaining sts on holder to be worked later.

Continue to work 15 (17, 19) sts of front in stockinette st (k one row, p one row) for 1 (1, 1.25) inch, ending on a WS row. Break off yarn, place sts on holder.

Reattach yarn to previously held sts and work in stockinette for 1 (1, 1.25) inch, slipping first st and knitting last st of each row to create selvedge, ending with WS row.

Next row: K across to end, cast on 7 (8, 9) sts using knitted cast on, k15 (17, 19) sts from holder, cast on 7 (8, 9) sts using knitted cast on, place marker for beginning of round. Join.
K in the round for 1 (1, 1) inch.

Body shaping

K 45 (51, 59) bind off 23 (27, 31), remove marker and continue to knit across to end of row – you will have 48 (54, 62) sts on needle and the bound-off sts should be centered over the two legholes. Turn work, slipping first st, and purl back. You are now working the piece flat. BO 2 sts at the beginning of the next 4 rows until you have 40 (46, 56) sts.

Decrease one st at each end of every other row until 34 (40, 44) sts remain.

Short-row shaping

Row 1: K to last 4 sts, wrap and turn.
Row 2: P to last 4 sts, wrap and turn.
Row 3: K to last 7 sts, wrap and turn.
Row 4: P to last 7 sts, wrap and turn. Place all 34 (40, 44) sts on a holder.

Body band

With CC1 and smaller needle, k across body sts from holder, then pick up 37 (41, 49) around rest of body opening so you have 71 (81, 93) sts. Place marker to indicate beginning of round and join work.
Work 5 rounds in k1, p1 ribbing.
Change to CC2. K one round, then do 1 round in k1, p1 ribbing as established.
Bind off in ribbing.

Leg bands

With CC1 and smaller needles, pick up 6 (7, 8) sts on each edge of leg hole for total of 24 (28, 32) sts. Work 5 rounds in k1, p1 ribbing. Change to CC2. K one round; then do one round in k1, p1 ribbing as established.

Finishing

Bind off in rib. Weave in ends.

Underneath view of completed Astro sweater.

Completed Astro sweater, side view.

Butter in sweater of hand-painted wool.

OLLY SWEATER

Sandy Stutz is a friend who is also an artist and successful businesswoman. She has, over the years, provided valuable advice about the function and style of the sweaters. I always knit a harness hole into my sweaters, having always used harnesses for my dogs. It was Sandy's idea to knit in a collar hole for dogs who are leashed to a collar. Sandy, a long-time dachshund companion, suggested that leg bands would be walked on by short-legged dogs. This sweater combines Sandy's ideas for a proper dachshund sweater, one that would be useful for any short-legged dog. A ribbed front panel provides ease, and the sweater is sleeveless for ease of movement. The sweater is named for Sandy's dog Olly, who, along with his sister Frieda Pixel, keeps Sandy company at work. Level: intermediate.

Finished size

▶ Neck: 10 (12, 14) inches. Chest: 16 (18, 20) inches. Finished length: 14 (16, 18) inches (excluding collar)

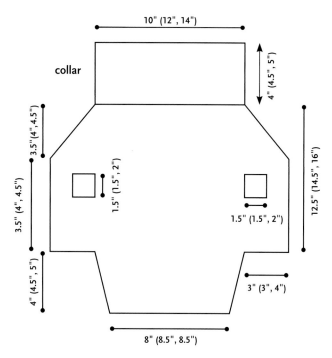

10" (12", 14")

collar

3.5" (4", 4.5")

3.5" (4", 4.5")

4" (4.5", 5")

1.5" (1.5", 2")

1.5" (1.5", 2")

4" (4.5", 5")

12.5" (14.5", 16")

3" (3", 4")

8" (8.5", 8.5")

Schematic of Olly sweater. Body band is not included.

Materials

▶ Worsted weight yarn: Main color (MC), 190 (220, 250) yards. Contrast color 1 (CC1), 100 (120, 150) yards. Contrast color 2 (CC2), 30 (40, 50) yards

▶ Size 5 (3.75 mm) and 6 (4.25 mm) needles

▶ Size 5 (3.75 mm) circular needle, 24 to 32 inches long

▶ 2 stitch holders if using straight needles for project

Gauge

▶ 18 stitches and 24 rows for 4 inches of stockinette stitch (k one row, p one row), using larger needles

DIRECTIONS

Collar

With CC2, using long-tail method, cast on 49 (59, 71) sts on circular or straight needles.

Row 1 (WS): Sl 1, p1, * k1, p1*, 4 (7, 9) times; place marker on needle, k3, *p3, k3*, 4 (4, 5) times; place marker on needle, p1, *k1, p1*, repeat to last st, k1.

Row 2 (RS): Slip 1, then k the k sts and p the p sts as they face you across row to last st, end k1.

Row 3: Repeat row 1.

Row 4: With CC1, k across.

Row 5: Repeat row 1.

Row 6: Repeat row 2.

Continue to repeat rows 1 & 2 with CC1 until collar measures 4 (4.5, 5) inches from beginning, ending with RS row. If collar hole is desired, bind off 3 center sts on last row.

Body

Row 1: With MC, and WS facing, sl 1, k across, casting on 3 sts at center if those sts were bound off in previous row (to complete

Butter and Peanut in their Olly sweaters.

Side view of finished Olly sweater showing bands and leg holes.

Underneath view of finished Olly sweater.

A collar closeup shows detail.

collar hole). Remove markers. At this point in the project, the WS of the collar is the RS of the body.

Row 2 (WS): Sl 1, p across, end k 1. (This creates a turning ridge between collar and body.)

Row 3: Sl 1, p1, *k1, p1* 7 times (16 sts worked), place marker, m1, k to last 17 sts, m1, place marker, *p1, k1* 8 times, end k1.

Row 4: Sl 1, continue k1, p1 rib as established to marker, p across center sts (stockinette st) to marker, resume k1, p1 rib, end k1.

Repeat rows 3 and 4, continuing to m1 every RS row after first marker and before 2nd marker, eleven more times until you have 73 (83, 95) sts on needle.

Leghole shaping

RS: Work 17 sts as established, bind off next 6 (6, 9) sts, work to last 23 (23, 26) sts, bind off next 6 (6, 9) sts, work remaining sts as established. Remove markers.

Three sections, divided by bound off sts, are now on needle. For a smooth leghole edge, maintain selvedge stitches by slipping the first st and knitting the last st on every row. You can work across each section individually, keeping the other sections on holders or on the cable of your circular needle, or you can attach 2 more balls of yarn and complete all three simultaneously. With MC yarn, continue in stock st until each section is 1.5 (1,5, 2) inches above leghole castoff, ending with WS row.

Optional: make harness hole using desired buttonhole method, in this section. (See techniques section for making buttonhole if needed.) Break yarn.

Re-join work (RS): On next row, work across each section as established and, using knitted cast on, CO6 (6, 9) sts between sections to complete legholes. Continue in stockinette st as established for 3 (4, 4.5) inches from leg cast on, ending with WS row.

Body shaping

Bind off 14 (14, 18) sts at beginning of next 2 rows.

RS: Sl 1, k1, ssk, k to last sts, k2 tog, k2.

WS: Sl 1, p to last st, k1.

Repeat decreases on RS every other row 5 more times, then every 4th row 1 (2, 4) times until 37 (39, 39) sts remain.

Work additional rows if needed, until piece measures 12 (14, 16) inches, ending with WS row.

Short-row shaping

RS: Work to last 3 sts, wrap and turn.

WS: Work as previous row.

RS: Work to last 6 sts, wrap and turn.

WS: Work to last 6 sts. Break yarn, placing all sts on holder. Sew center seam of sweater.

Body band

Using circular needle with CC1, k across sts on holder, knitting up wraps as they appear, then pick up 41 (49, 73) sts along edge of body, for total 78 (88, 112) sts.

Work in k1, p1 rib for 5 rounds.

Change to CC2, k one round. Work 1 round in rib as established. Bind off in rib.

To finish

Weave in ends.

A sleeveless sweater is a practical choice for a short-legged dog.

Peanut models a Frieda snood.

FRIEDA SNOOD

This little head covering was suggested by my friend Sandy Stutz. It can be tucked into a turtleneck or used alone to hold back long ears when your dog is eating. Short-row shaping on the crown helps keep the snood in place. Frieda Pixel is a tiny dachshund adopted by Sandy; Frieda can wear this snood when she accompanies her new sister Beila on a walk. Level: intermediate.

Finished size

▸ Width of snood: 6 (8, 10) inches. Length: 6 (6.5, 7.25) inches

Materials

▸ Worsted weight wool, 75 (100, 125) yards

▸ Size 4 (3.5 mm) double-pointed needles, l set

Gauge

▸ 24 sts and 40 rows for 4-inch square in mock rib (k1, p1 for one round, k next round)

65

Frieda Snood

DIRECTIONS

See techniques section for working in the round with double-pointed needles for guidance if needed.

Cast on 44 (56, 64) stitches; then divide them on three double-pointed needles as follows: 12 (16, 20) sts on needle #1; 20 (20, 24) sts on needle #2; 12 (16, 20) sts on needle #3. Join, and work 3 rounds in k2, p2, rib for 5 (5, 8) rounds.

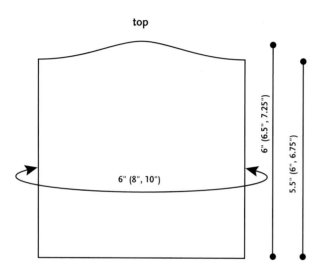

Frieda schematic.

Crown shaping

Work 12 (16, 20) sts on needle #1, 17 sts on needle #2, wrap and turn, work 12 sts, wrap and turn, work 8 sts, wrap and turn, work 6 sts, wrap and turn, ending with RS facing. Work across remaining sts on needle #2, knitting wraps together with established sts, complete round as established. Continue working rib until snood measures 2 (2, 2.25) inches from beginning, measuring from edge, excluding short rows.

Eyelet border

Purl one round, p1, yo for next round, purl one round. On next round, increase 12 (12, 16) sts, evenly spaced, for 60 (72, 80) sts. Work 1.5 (2, 2.5) inches in mock rib (k1, p1 for one round, k next round) and 1.5 (1.5, 2) inches in k1, p1, rib. Bind off in rib.

To finish

Weave in ends and block if needed.

The finished Frieda snood.

Frieda snood in profile view.

Zoey models a Cocoa hat.

COCOA HAT

A hat for a dog is a tricky thing. Dog heads are not shaped like ours. Then, there's the issue of the ears. Do we cover them or leave them exposed? There's always the chance that your pet won't tolerate a hat. For that pet, the Frieda snood might be a better choice. This hat has openings for ears and secures with long scarves that can wrap around a few times. Even with the scarf, this hat may only stay on long enough for you to snap that photo for your holiday card. I tried the finished product on Piccolo and got a few shots of her "I'm mad with you" look. I've named it for Cocoa, a sweet choco-late Lab who lives with my friends Yvette and Patrick and is a companion to their little boy, Spencer. Level: intermediate.

Finished size

▶ 8 inches around by 4 inches tall (10 inches around by 5 inches tall, 12 inches around by 6 inches tall)

Gauge

▶ 18 sts and 24 rows to 4 inches using larger size needles

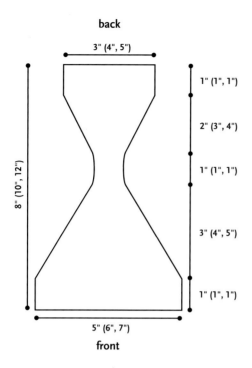

back

3" (4", 5")

1" (1", 1")

2" (3", 4")

1" (1", 1")

8" (10", 12")

3" (4", 5")

1" (1", 1")

5" (6", 7")

front

Cocoa schematic.

Materials

▸ Worsted weight yarn: Main color (MC), 50 (60, 70) yards. Contrast color 1 (CC1), 10 (23, 30) yards. Contrast color 2 (CC2), 10 (20, 30) yards

▸ Size 5 (3.75 mm) and 6 (4 mm) needles, or size to obtain gauge

▸ Pom-pom maker

▸ Yarn needle

▸ Crochet hook

DIRECTIONS FOR HAT

Front band

With smaller needle and CC2, cast on 28 (32, 36) stitches.

First row (WS): P1; then k1, p1 across, ending with k1.

Next row (RS): Sl 1, then work stitches as they appear across row, ending with k1. Break yarn.

WS: With CC1, sl 1, then p across to last stitch, and k last stitch. Starting with next RS row, work k1, p1 ribbing as established for 5 rows, ending with RS row. Maintain selvedges for entire hat construction by slipping first stitch and knitting last stitch of every row. Break yarn.

Hat crown

Changing to larger needle and stockinette st, with MC, on WS row, p across.

FRONT CROWN SHAPING

RS: Sl 1, k1, ssk, k to last 4 sts, k2tog, k2.

WS: Sl 1, p to last stitch, k1.

Repeat these two rows until 6 sts remain.

Work two more rows without shaping.

A completed Cocoa hat, with scarf attached.

BACK CROWN SHAPING

On next RS row: Sl 1, k2, m1, k to end (there should be 7 sts on needle at end).

WS: Sl 1, p to last stitch, k1.

RS: Sl 1, k3, m1, k to end (8 sts on needle).

WS: Sl 1, p to last st, k1.

BEGIN INCREASES

RS: Sl 1, k2, m1, k to last 3 sts, m1, k to end.

WS: Sl 1, p to last st, k1.

Repeat these two rows until there are 20 (24, 28) sts on needle, ending with RS row. Break yarn.

Back band

WS: Changing to smaller needle, with CC1, sl 1, p to last st, k1.

RS: Sl 1, *p1, k1*, repeat across row, ending with k1.

Work k1, p1 ribbing as established for 4 more rows, ending with RS row. Break yarn. With CC2, sl 1, p to last stitch, k1. Work 2 more rows in k1, p1 ribbing as established. Bind off. Block piece flat.

Hat assembly

With yarn needle, sew front to back at ribbed bands, leaving opening at sides for ears.

DIRECTIONS FOR ATTACHED SCARF

Pick up 3 (4, 5) sts on either side of hat seam on outer ribbed band (under ear hole) to start one length of scarf. Slipping first st of every row and knitting last st of every row, work in k1, p1, ribbing until scarf is 14 (16, 18) inches long. Bind off. Make the second length of the scarf on the other side of the hat in the same way.

Finishing

Using pom-pom maker and your choice of yarn, make one pom-pom and secure pom-pom to top of hat. Cut 5-inch lengths of yarn using your choice of colors and apply fringe to ends of scarves with a crochet hook. Trim fringe to desired length.

An assortment of Cocoa hats.

Mr. Lucky models a Cocoa hat.

Zeena (left) and Zoey in Libby kerchiefs.

LIBBY KERCHIEF

This scarf can be either cozy or glamorous, depending on your choice of fiber. Our samples are knit in wool and in a nylon ribbon that looks like suede. The scarf attaches to a purchased collar using a casing with a picot edge. Big dogs deserve some knitted love too, and if a sweater won't work, this stylish scarf is the answer. Liberty, also known as Libby, is a Weimaraner who keeps my friend Rachel company while she knits. The project is given in 3 sizes for small, medium and large dogs. Level: intermediate.

Finished size

▸ Approximately 8 inches wide by 4.5 inches long to point (10.5 by 5.5, 15 by 9); measure your dog's collar to determine the appropriate size to knit

Materials

▸ Worsted weight yarn, 40 (60, 80) yards

▸ Size 8 (5 mm) needle, or size that will obtain gauge

▸ Purchased dog collar

70

Gauge

▶ 16 sts and 20 rows to 4 inches in garter stitch

DIRECTIONS

Casing

Cast on 33 (41, 61) sts.

Slip first st and k last st of every row to maintain selvedge. Work in stockinette st (k1 row, p1 row) for 1 (1.25, 1.25) inch, ending with WS row.

Picot edge of casing: On next RS row, k1, *k2 tog, yo*, repeat across row.

To create back of casing: On next WS row, sl 1, p across to last st, k1. Continue in stockinette st for 1 (1.25, 1.25) inch after picot row, ending with WS row.

To close casing: As next RS row is being worked, carefully lift corresponding ridge from WS of each st of first row and knit it together with each stitch.

(Note: alternatively, the casing can be folded at the picot edge and sewn down after the scarf is complete.)

K all stitches on next row, eliminating selvedge stitch.

Shape scarf

Starting with RS row and on every row, k3, k2 tog, yo, k2 tog, k to end.

Repeat until 21 (25, 31) sts remain. You are working in garter st (k every row).

On every row, k3, k2 tog, yo, *k2tog*, twice, k to end.

Repeat until 13 (13, 15) sts remain.

Large size only: On next two rows, k3, k2tog, yo, k2 tog, k to end.

Three Libby scarves with their collars inserted.

To continue shaping, for all sizes

RS: K3, k2tog, yo, cdd, k to end.

WS: K across all WS rows to end.

RS: K3, k2tog, k1, k2tog, k3.

RS: K3, sl 1, k2tog, psso, k3.

RS: K2, sl 1, k2tog, psso, k2.

RS: K1, sl 1, k2 tog, psso, k1.

RS: Sl 1, k2tog, psso.

To finish

Weave in ends. Insert dog collar through casing.

Zeena models a Collar Cozy.

COLLAR COZY

I needed a knitted collar that would be a functional piece to restrain the dog. The Collar Cozy, a knitted tube that could add some style to a purchased simple collar, seemed right. The cozy slides over the buckle to eliminate irritation at the dog's neck. This project takes only a minimal amount of yarn. Smooth yarns work better for sliding the piece over the collar. Our samples were made using sport-weight wool yarn and a nylon ribbon yarn that resembles suede. Level: beginner.

Materials

- ▸ Yarn, less than 50 yards of desired weight (sport weight yarn used in sample)
- ▸ Double-pointed needles (2), or one short circular needle, in a size larger than what you would normally choose for your yarn
- ▸ Simple nylon or leather collar
- ▸ Yarn needle

Gauge

- ▸ Make a small swatch to determine how many stitches you are getting per inch

DIRECTIONS

Close collar to desired length and measure length. To determine how many stitches to cast on, multiply width of collar times 2, divide by how many stitches per inch, and add two stitches. For our samples, we cast on 8 stitches.

Knit every row, working loosely, without turning your work in the traditional sense. At the end of every row, slide stitches to the other end of the left-hand needle, or to the opposite end of your circular needle, and resume knitting with the first st of the row just worked. This creates a tube. The end stitch will be somewhat distorted, but that will correct after the cozy is fit to the collar.

Knit the tube to the desired length and bind off. If you want a gathered effect, knit the cozy 1.5 to 2 times the measured length. Weave in ends and work the finished tube over the collar, with one end on each side of the D-ring, pulling the cozy over the buckle after it is closed.

If you don't feel comfortable making a tube by this method, work stitches in stockinette stitch (k one row, p one row) to desired length, weave in ends, and whip stitch cozy around the collar.

Closeup of a Collar Cozy shows detail.

Unbuckled Collar Cozies.

Peanut and Butter sleeping in a Wally bed.

WALLY BED

What are your pets doing when you're away? More than likely, they're sleeping. What are they doing when you're home during the day? Sleeping. Knit your pet something cozy to sleep on.

This is a felted wool bed with some short-row shaping, and if the decreases look familiar, that's right, one end is a sock toe. This will create a sleeping cocoon to burrow into or, if your pet prefers to sleep on top, the double layer on one side will serve as a pillow. The garter stitch ridges add a little more cushion to the bed. I like a light felting for my objects, so you can still see that the piece was knit. If you prefer a more tightly felted bed, use larger needles, although this is likely to alter the yardage requirements. Wally is a little kitty who lives with my friends Bruce Mueller and Gary Wickland, who, like his siblings Max and Winnie, appreciates a woolly bed. Level: intermediate.

Finished size

▶ Approximately 36 by 22 inches before felting, 30 by 18 inches after felting

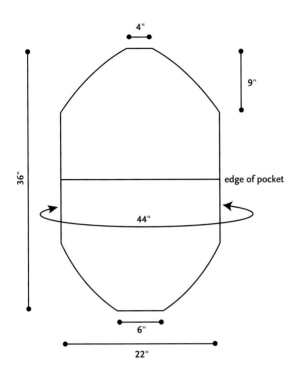

4"

9"

36"

edge of pocket

44"

6"

22"

Schematic for Wally bed.

DIRECTIONS

Cast on 40 sts on circular needle. Working back and forth in garter stitch (k every row), knit two rows.

Shape head of bed

K22, wrap and turn, k3, wrap and turn, k4 (knit wrap together with 4th stitch), wrap and turn, k5, wrap and turn, k6, wrap and turn, k7, wrap and turn, etc.

Continue working short rows in this manner, knitting one additional stitch at end of each short row and knitting together wraps with that last st as they appear, until you are again working across the entire 40 sts for the full row.

Continue to work piece in garter stitch until work measures 17 inches from beginning.

Create pocket

With working yarn, using knitted cast on method, CO 40 sts at the beginning of next row. Join all the work on the needle and the cast-on sts into the round (80 sts), placing markers at beginning and middle of round (at either end of the cast-on sts).

P1 round, k1 round to continue garter st in the round.

Repeat until work is 4 inches from cast on sts, ending with p round.

Materials

▸ Bulky weight wool yarn that will felt, approximately 470 yards

▸ Size 15 (10 mm) circular needle, 40 inches long

▸ Size 15 (10 mm) double-pointed needles, 1 set

▸ Yarn needle

Gauge

▸ 8 sts and 14 rows for 4 inches in garter stitch

Peanut in a Wally bed.

Pocket shaping

The pocket and the foot end of the bed are shaped simultaneously in one piece. Continuing in rounds of garter st, on next round k1, k2 tog, k to 3 sts before marker, ssk, k1, slip marker, k1, k2tog, slip marker, k to 3 sts before marker, ssk, k1.

P next round. It may be more comfortable at some point to transfer stitches to double-pointed needles as rounds get smaller.

Repeat these two rounds until 12 sts remain, continuing to decrease one st as established on either side of each marker.

Divide on two double-pointed needles and BO purlwise, using three-needle bind off. (See techniques section of the book for guidance.) Weave in ends to finish.

Felting

To felt, place bed in pillowcase and secure top. Wash in machine, using hot water, and a small amount of mild detergent. Rinse with cold water, checking work to make sure it does not felt more than desired. Repeat this process if necessary until bed is size desired. Let bed air-dry before use.

The finished Wally bed.

Lyubi peeking out of his blanket.

L Y U B I   B L A N K E T

Piccolo's favorite place when I'm knitting is curled up next to me. I had an alpaca cowl that I had knit on the sofa one day and, being the fiber-loving creature she is, she chose to nap on it. I thought a little blanket in a luscious fiber would be just the perfect accessory. Knit in garter stitch, it looks good on both sides and has a sawtooth edge to keep things interesting. The shape ends up being on the bias and is a little off kilter. The ridges of the garter stitch make for a cushy and cozy doggie wrap. I used alpaca for my samples, but it can be knit in any fiber you choose. Alpaca is as soft as cashmere, but not nearly as pricy. For easy care, the blanket would be nice in a superwash bulky wool. The small size is just enough to take in a pet carrier or cover a curled up little dog. The larger size would double nicely as a stroller blanket for a two-legged baby or as a lovely lap robe. I named the blanket for one of the models in the book, Lyubi (pronounced Loo-bee) whose name in Russian means "love." He chose, nine years ago, as a puppy, to have Lonnie Leonard as his companion; seeing their connection to each other was one of the highlights of the photo shoot. Level: beginner.

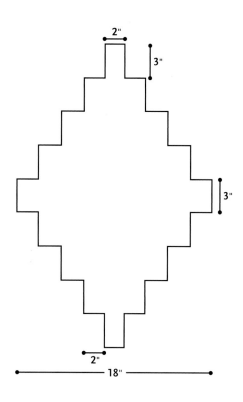

Lyubi schematic

Finished size

▶ 18 by 27 (30 by 45) inches

Materials

▶ Bulky weight yarn, 230 (450) yards

▶ Size 10.5 (6.5 mm) circular needle, 32 inches long

▶ Yarn needle

Gauge

▶ 12 sts and 22 rows for 4 inches in garter stitch

DIRECTIONS

The blanket is made all in one piece and is knit flat. The first half uses cast ons to increase stitches until the blanket gets to the desired width; the second half of the blanket uses bind offs to taper it down. A circular needle with a long cable is suggested to support the number of stitches at the widest point, but not absolutely necessary.

First half (increasing)

Cast on 9 sts using knitted cast on. Knit every row for 12 rows. *At beginning of next two rows, cast on 9 sts. Knit every row for 10 rows.* Repeat these 12 rows 4 (6) times until 99 (135) sts are on needle.
Knit 12 rows.

Bee under a Lyubi blanket.

Second half (decreasing)

Cast off 9 sts at beginning of next two rows. Knit 10 rows.
Repeat these 12 rows 4 (6) times, until 9 sts remain.
Knit 11 rows; bind off.

To finish

Weave in ends.

Lyubi blanket in variegated yarn.

The outspread blanket.

Lyubi blanket also makes a good stroller blanket.

Woodie, playing with a Chickies toy.

CHICKIES TOY

Piccolo loves the squeak toys. She's the first dog I've had that plays with toys, and I get a kick out of watching her run around with a little toy in her mouth. I love hearing the happy squeaky sound when I'm in another room in the house. This toy combines the squeak with a shape of a favorite dog food in my house, the chicken leg. This project used worsted yarn, knit on small needles in a tight gauge to hold the stuffing in. The yarn should felt a little after the toy has been played with. Cats like chicken, too! You can stuff with toy with catnip for some kitty fun. Level: beginner.

- 5 inches circumference by 7 inches long (8 by 8 inches)

Materials

- Worsted weight yarn, approximately 50 (75 yards)
- Size 4 (3.5 mm) needles
- Polyester stuffing
- Squeaker (available at pet supply stores)
- Yarn needle

80

Next row (RS): Sl 1, *k1, m1*, repeat to last 3 (2) sts, k3 (2) for a total of 31 (48) sts.

Work stockinette for 21 (29) rows, ending with WS.

Next row (RS): Sl 1, k2tog across row, end k1.

WS: Sl 1, p to last st, k1.

Repeat the previous two rows until 4 sts remain. Break off 12 inches of yarn and pull through remaining sts.

To finish

Sew sides together from the top down, stuff toy, and place squeaker at widest end of toy. Weave in ends.

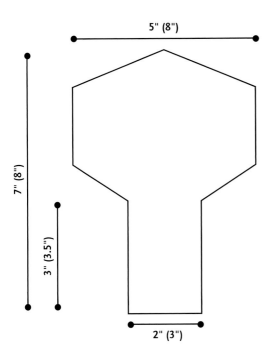

Chickies schematic.

Serving up some Chickies toys.

Gauge

▶ 6 sts and 7 rows to 1 inch in stockinette stitch (k one row, p one row)

DIRECTIONS

Cast on 12 (18) sts. Slipping the first st and knitting the last st of every row, knit 3 inches in stockinette st, ending with WS row.

Shaping

RS: Sl 1, *k1, m1*, repeat to last st, k1 for a total of 22 (35) sts. Work stockinette st for 5 (7) rows, ending with WS.

One for the road.

YODA SWEATER

I took a class from Vivian Hoxbro and asked her to sign her book, *Domino Knitting*. She wrote, "There is no dog sweater in this book, but you can create one." This sweater, worked one diamond at a time, is a good use for self-striping yarns or as a memory sweater with scraps of yarn used in some of your favorite sweaters. Mix textures for a crazy-quilt effect. Size can be adjusted for bigger dogs by using a heavier yarn, bigger needles, and making the individual diamonds bigger. Take time, while you knit the sweater, to weave in ends as you go, so you don't make yourself crazy at the end. This sweater is named for my first dog, Yoda, who is the original catalyst for my sweater designs. Level: advanced.

Finished size

▸ Neck: 9 (11, 12, 13, 14, 15) inches. Chest: 14 (15, 19, 20, 22, 25) inches. Length: 10 (12, 15, 17, 19, 22) inches (excluding collar)

Gauge

▸ On size 6 needles, diamond is 2 (2.25, 2.75, 3, 3.25, 4) inches across widest part of diamond, from end loop diagonally to opposite point

Materials

- ▶ Worsted weight yarn, 175 (220, 250, 300, 450, 550) yards, in self-striping yarn or in a variety of colors

- ▶ Sizes 5 (3.75 mm) and 6 (4.25 mm) double-pointed needles

- ▶ Size 5 (3.75 mm) circular needle, 24 inches long

- ▶ Scrap yarn or safety pins for stitch holders

- ▶ Yarn needle

DIRECTIONS

Foundation diamonds

The finished length of the side of a foundation diamond is the total number of stitches cast on minus one stitch, divided in half. Our foundation diamond has a 13 total stitches cast on, so the length of the side ends up being 6 stitches (13-1 = 12; 12 divided by 2 = 6). The diamond is shaped by the effect of the center decreases. You'll need to make 5 foundation diamonds. Here are the instructions for one foundation diamond (Fig. 1). Using double-pointed needles, cast on 13 (15, 17, 19, 21, 25) sts by knitted cast on.

Row 1 (WS): Sl 1, k to end.
Row 2 (RS): Sl 1, k4 (5, 6, 7, 8, 10), sl 1, k2 tog, psso, k5 (6, 7, 8, 9, 11).
Row 3, and all odd-numbered rows: Repeat row 1.
Row 4: Sl 1, k3 (4, 5, 6, 7, 8, 9), sl 1, k2 tog, psso, k4 (5, 6, 7, 8, 10).
Repeat center decrease as established on all even-numbered rows, until 3 sts remain, k across row, turn work, sl 1, k2 tog, psso, ending with one live stitch, break yarn. Put remaining stitch on a piece of scrap yarn. The live stitch will be used later as the center stitch of the diamond that is being created above it. This completes foundation diamond #1.

Repeat 4 times for a total of 5 loose foundation diamonds in colors of your choice. They will be 1F, 2F, 3F, 17F, and 18F diamonds on the charts.

Fig. 1 Begin the sweater with by creating 5 loose foundation diamonds like this one. Note that last stitch has been left loose, so it can be knitted in later on.

Other diamonds

Except for the foundation diamonds, each of the rest of the diamonds is created and attached at the same time. Half the stitches are cast on with the new diamond's yarn, one stitch is picked up from the corner of an existing diamond or using the live stitch from the corner below, and half the stitches are picked up from the side of an existing diamond.

Follow charts for creating diamonds, creating/joining them in numerical order.

Kinds of diamond

The following are explanations of diamond codes on the charts:

F (Foundation) Diamonds. These are the five loose diamonds that you create first.

C (Center) Diamonds. On C diamonds, stitches are picked up from two sides of the diamonds below the center diamond (Fig. 2 and 3).

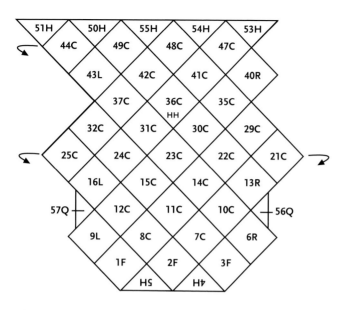

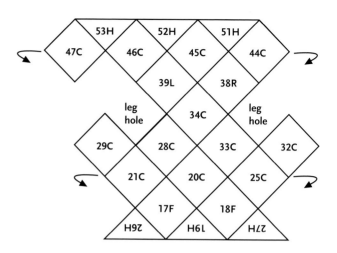

Yoda chart 1 Start with three foundation diamonds (1F, 2F, 3F) and create/attach the other diamonds in numerical order, ending with 16L. If type is upside down, turn work while creating that half-diamond.

Yoda chart 2 Start with two foundation diamonds (17F and 18F), and create/attach the other diamonds in numerical order, turning work upside down in direction of label if indicated. 21C joins the two separate pieces of diamonds together, and 25C joins the two into the round. The same number may appear on both charts, but each diamond is worked only once.

L (Left-Attached) Diamonds. Half the stitches (6 for smallest size) are picked up from the left side of the diamond below the one you're creating (this will become the lower right edge of the new diamond). A stitch is taken through the corner where the diamonds will come together. Then what will become the lower left side of the new diamond is created by casting on 6 stitches (for smallest size) using the knitted cast on (Fig. 4).

R (Right-Attached) Diamonds. Cast on the specified number of stitches (6 for smallest size), using the knitted cast on, for what will become the right side of the new diamond; pick up one stitch at the corner where the diamonds come together; pick up 6 (or specified number) of stitches from the upper right side of the diamond below the new diamond; the 6 stitches will become the lower left side of the new diamond (Fig. 6).

H: Half-Diamonds. They are actually triangles half the size of a diamond. See directions below.

Q: Quarter Diamonds. See directions on page 86.

Use small lengths of scrap yarn to hold live stitches left from half and quarter diamonds.

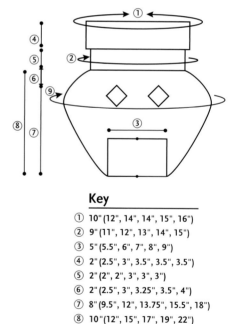

Key

① 10" (12", 14", 14", 15", 16")
② 9" (11", 12", 13", 14", 15")
③ 5" (5.5", 6", 7", 8", 9")
④ 2" (2.5", 3", 3.5", 3.5", 3.5")
⑤ 2" (2", 2", 3", 3", 3")
⑥ 2" (2.5", 3", 3.25", 3.5", 4")
⑦ 8" (9.5", 12", 13.75", 15.5", 18")
⑧ 10" (12", 15", 17", 19", 22")
⑨ 14" (15", 19", 20", 22", 25")

Yoda sweater schematic. Body band is not included.

Fig. 2 To make a center diamond (here, blue yarn), stitches were picked up on the side of what will be the two nearest diamonds below it. In this case, they are two loose foundation diamonds.

Fig. 3 The completed blue center diamond.

- ▶ Diamonds 1 through 16 are worked for one section. Begin with 6R, then work 7C and 8C to 9L to complete one row of diamonds, moving from right to left on the chart to join foundation diamonds 1F through 3F.

- ▶ Half diamonds 4H and 5H can be knit in their numbered order.

- ▶ Work diamonds 17 through 20 to create another section. Join 17F and 18F, using 19H to begin.

- ▶ Diamond 21 joins the two sections you just created.

- ▶ Diamond 25 joins the sweater into the round.

- ▶ Diamond 44C joins diamonds 38R and 43L to close one leg hole. Diamond 46C joins 39L to 40R to close the other leg hole.

You can see a new right-attached diamond being added in Figs. 5 and 6. Figures 2 and 7 show a center diamond being added.

Figure 8 shows a close-up of the Yoda sweater diamonds in lavenders and blues.

To make half-diamonds (H)

To create a half-diamond, pick up a total of 13 (15, 17, 19, 21, 25) stitches from the two diamonds below: 6 (7, 8, 9, 10, 12) from each diamond below, plus the live stitch left from diamond below for the center stitch. (If you are working from an edge that has no live stitch, pick up an additional stitch in the corner of one of the diamonds.) For example, pick up 6 stitches from diamond 3F, the live stitch from 7C, and six stitches from 2F to start half-diamond 4H. Then:

Row 1, and all odd number rows (WS): Sl 1, k to end.

Row 2 (RS): Sl 1, ssk, k2 (3, 4, 5, 6, 8), sl 1, k2tog, psso, k2 (3, 4, 5, 6, 8), k2 tog, k1. You will have 9 (11, 13, 15, 17, 21) sts on needle.

Row 4: Sl 1, ssk, k 0 (1, 2, 3, 4, 6), sl 1, k2tog, psso, k2tog, k 0 (1, 2, 3, 4, 6), k2tog, k1. You will have 5 (7, 9, 11, 13, 17) sts.

Continue to decrease in this manner on either end of row, and over center 3 sts (k2 tog, psso) until 5 (7, 7, 7, 9, 9) sts remain. Then on next RS row dec only over center 3 sts (sl 1, k2tog, psso). 3 (5, 5, 5, 7, 7) sts remain. Finish with one WS row. Place remaining live sts from half-diamonds on holders when done with half-diamond.

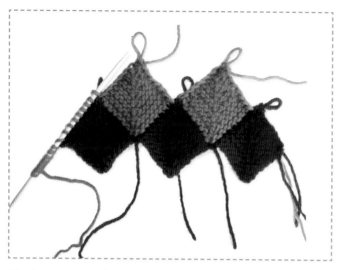

Fig. 4 Creating a new left-attached (L) diamond. Half the total number of stitches needed are picked up from left side of the diamond below.

Fig. 5 Creating a new, right-attached diamond, using knitted cast on method. Cast on half the number of stitches needed for the right side of the new diamond. The live stitch remaining from the diamond below (red in photo) is used for the center stitch, then the rest of the stitches needed are picked up along the right edge of the diamond that will be to the left of the new diamond (blue in photo). The picked-up stitches will become the lower left edge of the new diamond.

Quarter diamonds (Q)

The quarter diamonds fill in the space between a full and half-diamond so the body band can be added later. Refer to the charts for their placement. Choose the instructions below for your pattern size.

QUARTER DIAMOND 56Q
(for 3 smaller sizes of sweater)

Pu a total of 10 sts, 5 at diamond 6R and 5 at diamond 26H.

Row 1 and all WS rows: Sl 1, k to end.
Row 2: Sl 1, ssk, sl 1, k2tog, psso, k2.
Row 4: Sl 1, ssk, sl 1, k2tog, psso, k1.

After working row 5, place the remaining 4 sts on holder.

QUARTER DIAMOND 56Q
(for 3 larger sizes of sweater)

Pu 13 sts at diamonds 6R and 26H, 6 on each side, and pick up the odd stitch in the corner as well.

Row 1 and all WS rows: Sl 1, k to end.
Row 2: Sl 1, ssk, k1, sl 1, k2tog, psso, k3, k2tog, k1.
Row 4: Sl 1, sl 1, k2tog, psso, k2, k2tog, k1.

After completing row 5, place remaining 6 sts on holder.

QUARTER DIAMOND 57Q
(for 3 smaller sizes of sweater)

Pu 10 sts at diamonds 27H and 9L, 5 on each side.

Row 1 and all WS rows: Sl 1, k to end.
Row 2: Sl 1, k1, sl 1, k2tog, psso, k1.
Row 4: Sl 1, sl 1, k2tog, psso, k2tog, k1.

After working row 5, place 4 sts on holder.

QUARTER DIAMOND 57Q
(for 3 larger sizes of sweater)

Pu 13 sts at diamonds 27H and 9L: 6 sts on each side and one in the corner in between.

Row 1 and all WS rows: Sl 1, k to end.
Row 2: Sl 1, ssk, k3, sl 1, k2tog, psso, k1, k2tog, k1.
Row 4: Sl 1, ssk, k2, sl 1, k2tog, psso, k1.

After working row 5, place 6 remaining sts on holder.

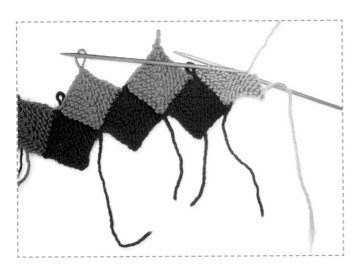

Fig. 6 Adding a right-attached diamond (for another Yoda sweater).

Fig. 7 Adding a center diamond.

Fig. 8 Close-up of another Yoda sweater, showing diamonds.

Neck

Using circular needle, starting in center front, with the live stitch left after completing diamond 45C, pu sts, evenly spaced, knitting the live sts left on holders from the half-diamonds and single sts left from whole diamonds. Count sts on needle, and k one round increasing or decreasing, evenly spaced, as necessary for 52 (60, 68, 76, 80, 84) sts. Figure 9 shows the completed neck and collar.

Note: For neck, stitches should be a multiple of 4 for k2, p2 rib, or alternatively, a multiple of 2 for a k1, p1 rib. If you have an odd number of stitches after picking up around the neck, correct this by either increasing or decreasing in the first round to the desired number of stitches.

Work k2, p2 rib for 2 (2, 2, 3, 3, 3) inches, then garter st (k one round, p one round) for 2 (2.5, 3, 3.5, 3.5, 3.5) inches. Bind off.

Optional picot bind off: *Cast on 2 sts to left-hand needle using knitted cast on, bind off 4 sts*. Repeat for entire round.

Leg bands

Using smaller double-pointed needles, pick up 6 (7, 7, 8, 8, 8) sts on each of 4 edges of open diamonds (around leg hole). Some live stitches may be found; either tie them off or work them into the leg band stitches. Work in garter stitch (k one round, p next round) for 5 (5, 5, 9, 9, 9) rounds. Bind off on p round. You can see a closeup of the leg bands in Figure 9.

Body band

Beginning with live sts in diamond 19H, using smaller circular needle, pick up 86 (94, 100, 102, 104, 106) sts, knitting live sts as they appear. Work in garter stitch (k1 round, p1 round) for 5 (5, 5, 9, 9, 9) rounds. On knit rounds, k2tog at 19H, 56Q and 57Q on the chart and at the corners of 1F and 3F diamonds. Bind off on p round.

Note: To add an accent color to the sweater, work 2 rounds in contrast color, creating one garter stitch ridge in collar, body and leg bands.

To finish

Weave in ends. Block or steam if necessary. Figure 10 shows the completed sweater.

Fig. 9 Close-up of collar and half-diamonds.

Fig. 10 The finished Yoda sweater, seen from the side.

About the Author

I taught myself to knit as a child and have never stopped. After decades of knitting for myself and family, something changed when I adopted my first dog—I had to knit for her. Knitting dog garments continued with the dogs that followed, until I reached the point where I imagined what every dog I met would look like when wearing something hand-knit. Lucky Penny Hand Made (www.luckypennyhandmade.com) was the little business that grew from my apartment to the Internet, and to craft fairs and fiber shows.

My background includes theatrical costume design and photo styling. In fact, I styled the photography in this book. I reside in Chicago with my dog Piccolo, who provides inspiration for future designs.

Corinne Niessner
Chicago, Illinois

US AND METRIC NEEDLE SIZES

US	Metric	US	Metric
0	2 mm	6	4 mm
1	2.25 mm	7	4.5 mm
2	2.75 mm	8	5 mm
3	3.25 mm	9	5.5 mm
4	3.5 mm	10	6 mm
5	3.75 mm	10 1/2	6.5 mm

METRIC EQUIVALENTS CHART

(to the nearest mm and 0.1 cm)

inches	mm	cm	inches	mm	cm
1/8	3	0.3	2.5	64	6.4
1/4	6	0.6	3	76	7.6
3/8	10	1.0	3.5	89	8.9
1/2	13	1.3	4	102	10.2
5/8	16	1.6	4.5	114	11.4
3/4	19	1.9	5	127	12.7
7/8	22	2.2	6	152	15.2
1	25	2.5	7	178	17.8
1.25	32	3.2	8	203	20.3
1.5	38	3.8	9	229	22.9
1.75	44	4.4	10	254	25.4
2	51	5.1			

Index